# THE DIVINE EMBRACE

# THE DIVINE EMBRACE

## DISCOVERING THE REALITY OF GOD'S LOVE

CHRISTINA REES

DARTON·LONGMAN+TODD

Published in 2006 by
Darton, Longman and Todd Ltd
1 Spencer Court
140–142 Wandsworth High Street
London
SW18 4JJ

First published in 2000 by Fount, an imprint of HarperCollins*Publishers*
This revised and updated edition published in 2006

ISBN 0 232 52623 0

A catalogue record for this book is available from the British Library.

Printed and bound in Great Britain by
CPI Bath

*To my beloved daughters*
*Angela and Alexandra –*
*this one's for you,*
*with all my love.*

# CONTENTS

# ACKNOWLEDGEMENTS

So many people have helped to bring this book about. My first thanks are to David Stone, who asked me several years ago whether I would like to write a book on some aspect of what I believe. David started the whole process, and for that I am very grateful. I am also grateful to James Catford, who gave me steady encouragement and sound advice. Most of all, he helped me to focus on what I really want to say about a loving God. More recently, I am so grateful to Virginia Hearn who inspired and made possible this new edition published by Darton, Longman and Todd.

I would like to extend special thanks to David Lloyd, who by his encouragement, generosity and vision has helped to make this book, and so much else, possible. My thanks also to all those involved with The Churchfield Trust: your support and wisdom are much appreciated.

I owe a huge debt to my husband Chris, who always gives me excellent and rigorous feedback, and who has never allowed a computer to swallow my words for good! I thank him most of all for his love and belief in me, and for communicating day in and day out a deep understanding of the God who is Love.

My thanks also to so many wonderful friends who have encouraged me more than they will ever know by their enthusiasm and prayerful support. I particularly want to thank Ros Holbrow, whose friendship, humour and courage have helped me to see the love of God at work in new ways, and Sarah Smith, whose quiet love in action and dry wit over the past 24 years has brought me much comfort and joy.

I would like to thank my distant family and friends, whose love spans oceans and continents and times. They have helped me to realise that there is no distance between us when we are joined together in the One who is Love.

Lastly, I would like to thank my mother, Carol Benton Muller, who was the first person to show me the human face of our loving God. Her courage, steadfastness and unshakeable faith helped to set me on the pilgrim's path, and her love for me has given me the strength to follow Christ, wherever he has led me.

To you all, my thanks and my love.

Christina Rees
January 2005

## INTRODUCTION

I could not worship a God who did not love me. I could not respond with love to a God I couldn't trust. The God I find emerging from the pages of the Bible, and who I read about in the lives of the saints, is one of love. I also find evidence for the God of love in my own life and in the lives of many of my friends, but I and many others have a problem with the concept of unconditional love. Does it exist, and if so, where?

If God is love, and is responsible for making us and the whole universe, then it might be worthwhile taking a closer look at God. The only way we can know God is through our own experience. Of course we can learn about God from the Bible, other books, art and talking to other people, but the only way to know God, to have a sense of God's reality, is by embarking on a personal journey of discovery. Some people have begun with intellectual head trips, others with outward rituals, but, ultimately, for God to mean anything more than just a nice idea or a worthy concept, it has to get personal.

The Bible, the definitive Christian source book, makes an amazing claim about God. It doesn't just say that God is loving, or that God has done loving acts; it states boldly that 'God is love' (1 John 4:8). What does that really mean, and what are we supposed to do about it?

This book is an attempt to answer some of these and other questions about God, and to explain why I can say, and trust, that God is love. I don't think any of us ever gets all the answers during our lives, but I am confident that we can come to accept that certain things are true. There will always be a tentativeness in any writing about God. It will always be the case that the full picture is bigger than we can ever see, but at least some of what we can see can be clear, and tell us more about what we cannot see.

For a time, I was so desperate to get life 'right' and to be considered good by God, that I was fiercely strict with myself. I searched high and low for the key to the secret of life, the little elusive piece of the jigsaw that would make everything else fall into place. But now I don't see life, or God, or myself, like that. And if I have discovered anything, it's probably that I had the key to life with me all the time, only I didn't trust myself enough to believe it.

So what is the key to life, the secret to the universe? I believe that it is seeing and acting upon the truth that God is love, love reaching out to us. The secret is about learning to respond to God's love, and taking the risk of sharing it with other people. I think it is only through love that we develop the eyes to see the world, each other and ourselves the way God sees us. It is only through love that we can please God and have the courage to live our lives in ways which are not ultimately pointless, destructive or boring. It is only with love that we can accept our full humanity and the humanity of others. It is only with love that we can face some of the horrors of life, and still persevere in hope and joy. It is only with love that we can stop fooling ourselves that we either do, or have to, know it all. Following God, following love, is what can keep us going when we would rather pull up the covers and never again climb out from under them. It's scary, difficult and frustrating at times, but I believe it's worth it.

I believe that I can write about God's love only to the extent that I have accepted and experienced it. I could have chosen to trace the story of God's love in the life of Jesus, or in other people's lives throughout history, and that might have been a worthwhile exercise. But I wanted to write from the position of one who is living, and testing, what I am writing.

I actually think that the story of God's love is a story we are all living. Some of us are resisting, some responding timidly, and some boldly. Some don't yet know how to make sense of the story, and some don't even believe there is a story to tell. The best analogy I can think of is to compare God's love with the bright noonday sun. We can choose to lie out in it, or go and find shade somewhere, or even stay indoors and pull the curtains shut. We can even fail to see the sun because of thick layers of clouds. But whatever we do, or whatever we can or cannot see, the sun is still shining. Like all analogies, this one fails if pressed too far, but it does speak of the constant reality of God's love, and of our choices in response to it. The sun can only ever shine down on us while the God of love creates us, comes into us and can shine out of us from within.

Believing in love requires trusting and taking risks, and we need to 'risk the holy terror of living as if love really mattered'.[1] In that holy terror we can discover the reality of God's love and find ourselves to be held close in the Divine Embrace.

# In the Beginning

Once when I woke up early one morning in May, on our little smallholding in Hertfordshire, I saw nature as if for the first time. It was warm and the sun had risen, but there was still a soft mist nestling in the curves of the valley and surrounding the trees with a light haze. Drops of dew glistened on the leaves of the bushes, and everything seemed fresh and new. I listened to the birds singing, and watched a rabbit nibbling grass in a corner of the garden. I caught sight of a squirrel performing aerial gymnastics in between the willow and the walnut trees. The air was filled with the scent of apple blossom and lilac.

Still rather sleepy, I moved as if on auto-pilot. I got dressed, went downstairs, had my usual love-in with the dogs, wiped off dog saliva, let dogs out, let cats in, fed them all, put out maize for the chickens, and made myself a fresh pot of coffee. This morning it was so warm that I left the kitchen door open, thereby risking chicken-in-the-kitchen invasion, and forgot to turn on the radio.

Completely without warning, I found myself singing the words of the old hymn, 'Morning has broken', which seemed to have been written for that day: '. . . blackbird has spoken like the first bird . . .' I was acutely conscious of being alive, of being part of an amazingly varied and extraordinarily beautiful creation. I stood outside, bathed in the soft sunlight, and thanked God for creating such beauty, for letting me experience it, and for giving me life.

You see, I believe in a loving God. More than that, I believe in a God who *is* love, about whom nothing better, nothing higher, nothing truer can be said than 'God is love'. I believe this God created all existence in a cosmic explosion of overflowing love. The overabundance of God's love created a space that held within it the possibility of relationship with others. I believe that space is our universe, and that we humans have within us a special capacity for relating to God, similar to, and yet different from, for instance, how we might love dogs, cats or chickens.

I also believe that part of God's overpowering urge to create was the element of longing. Perhaps it is valid to say that we have always existed in God's mind, dreamed up by God before we ever existed in space and time. The universe may have taken billions of years to produce life on earth, but all that time God kept the dream of us alive. We exist because God longed for the possibility of including others in the Godhead of love. I don't mean to imply that there was anything lacking in God's Being, but there was a wild dream of the possibility of loving more, of including others in that love, a possibility worth the risk of creation. Above, beyond and yet somehow including the greenness of my garden and the enthusiasm of my dogs, my reality is based on my faith in and my experience of God's love: I am loved, therefore I am.

I had what might be described as an alternative childhood. For most of my formative years I lived with my family on a small wooden sailboat, the *Tappan Zee*, travelling up and down the East Coast of America and in the Caribbean and Mediterranean seas. My father, John Muller Jr, who had been a talent scout for Oxford University Press, and my mother, Carol Benton Muller, who had been a teacher, left their jobs, sold our house, gave away our lovely cocker spaniel named Telemachus, and started an entirely new lifestyle with their three young children.

When we first sailed out of a New York harbour and into our new life, my sister Robin was seven, my brother Joel was four, and I was five. My parents had to keep us strapped up in puffy orange life jackets so that if we fell overboard we would float. I was partial at the time to a pair of very cool shades, and a set of brightly coloured, plastic, snap-together alphabet letters, which I carried everywhere with me, just in case. I never knew when I might feel a word coming on.

One of my earliest memories is of sitting up on the deck of the boat at night, just before going down below to our bunks. Away from towns and cities, with only a few smoky oil lanterns, we could see the stars as if they were hanging from the rigging. My mother would point out the constellations and teach us their names – the seven sisters of the Pleiades, Cassiopeia, the big and little dippers, and my favourite, Orion and his belt. I think he was my favourite because he was the easiest to recognise. I can remember countless nights of staring into the sky, hypnotised by the stars and planets and lulled by the gentle rocking of the boat.

During the times when we were sailing out of sight of land it was possible to see 360 degrees around us of uninterrupted sea and sky. I don't know how old I was when I started to imagine that the sky was a huge blue bowl, empty except for clouds and wind, turned upside down on top of the ocean, another huge bowl, filled to the brim, and sometimes sloshing over. I would picture our boat as a tiny dot, sailing across an eternity of sea under an infinity of sky.

As we would sit and take turns at the tiller or coil ropes and polish brass, I would ask my mother, the resident theologian, 'How did God make the sky and the ocean?' and she would answer, 'He just did. Because he's God.' And then I would ask, 'How did God begin?' and my mother would say, 'He never began. He's always existed.' 'But what existed before God?' 'There was no *before* God.'

We would go on like this for hours, wrestling with the ontology of the Divine as well as the meatier issues of why sharks and mosquitoes bite, and why birds can fly but humans can't. (I've always had a little bone to pick with God about the fact that we didn't get the wings.) My mother was endlessly patient with us, and these discussions became part of our everyday discourse. We said grace before every meal, and had a time of family prayers every night, with each of us adding something. We would finish with the Lord's prayer and then sing a few hymns, each of us getting to choose our favourites.

The God I worshipped then was primarily God the Creator and Sustainer. I knew who kept my brother from being eaten by the alligators when he fell overboard, I knew who was responsible for protecting us during the hurricanes, and I was sure who I had to thank when accidents were averted and storms failed to reach us. I was aware of Jesus, whom I saw as a kindly, but rather quiet, older brother, and I was a bit hazy about the Holy Spirit, whom I think I imagined as second cousin to a whirlwind.

My understanding of the universe and God may have progressed significantly since those childhood chats with my mother, but the *how* and the *what* at the heart of the universe is still a mystery, even though thanks to the Hubble space telescope we now know so much more. We have learned that the universe is even more vast than we had thought, containing at least 50 billion more galaxies than had previously been estimated. What is more, an analysis of some of Hubble's more recent information suggests that the universe is around 9 billion years old, half as old as other calculations had determined.

The Bible suggests that God came first and started the whole thing off. In the beginning, there was nothing but God. The writer of Genesis, the first book of the Bible, takes the existence of God for granted, and begins with God's act of creation, an act that unfolds over six days. After each day God is pleased and sees that what he has created is good. On the fifth day, after God has created sea creatures and winged fowl, God blesses what he has made and says to all the fish and birds, 'be fruitful and multiply'. The Creator God not only acts, but reacts, and his first reactions are those of delight at the work of his hands: 'And God saw that it was good.' Creation, delight and blessing; the first gifts of God to the world he has made.

How the world was made is a question that has obsessed people throughout history. Most religions and cultures have their own explanations of how, and why, the world began, some more colourful and fanciful to our eyes than others. Scientists now quibble over the exact date, give or take a few billion years, of the Big Bang, the explosion at the beginning of time that is thought to have started off life as we know it. Nobody knows exactly what happened, when it happened, how it happened, or why it happened, but there is a general consensus that it did happen.

What astronomers and other scientists have discovered is important, because it affects our understanding of aspects of what we believe. Over the years science has influenced what we believe, and at some points, science has recognised the mystery of God in the structure and design of reality. Einstein stated that 'Religion without science is blind. Science without religion is lame.' John Polkinghorne, the scientist and priest, would rather say that 'Religion without science is confined; it fails to be completely open to reality. Science without religion is incomplete; it fails to attain the deepest possible understanding.'[1]

Christianity has, alas, been guilty of failing to be completely open to reality. Remember Galileo. Galileo was an Italian astronomer and physicist who reasoned that the planets must move around the sun. He wrote a book explaining his theory and found himself hauled before the Inquisition, accused of heresy. At the time, the Church believed that the earth was at the centre of the universe and to say otherwise was not a life- or career-enhancing move. Galileo was found guilty and banned from writing and teaching. He saved his skin by recanting (but under his breath he still believed) and was sentenced to life imprisonment. Happily, he was still fairly well respected, and so he was allowed to live under house arrest until he died.

Even today, there are those who believe that Earth was made by God in six 24-hour periods, just as Genesis describes it. There are also those whose reading of the Bible leads them to believe that the six days of creation took place less than ten thousand years ago. These people claim that fossils in the rocks are not the ossified remains of ancient creatures now extinct, but rather that God created fossils *as* fossils and put them in the rock.

We may raise our eyebrows at those who think like this, we may even call them unkind names; but there is one thing that most Christians do tend to agree on: all there is to life, even all that can be detected or surmised about outer space, everything there is was made, one way or another, by God. And if new worlds are discovered spinning in farthest outer space, these, too, have been made by God. We may bicker about the *how* of it, but I think Christians are in general agreement that God created us and all there is.

A few years ago an article in the *Sunday Times Magazine*, stated:

> Hubble may help us to look not only backwards but forwards, to deduce whether humanity really does have a future out there among the stars, whether one day we may indeed boldly go where no one has gone before. In the meantime, it proved that God still has the best special effects.[2]

For some people, though, it is hard enough to believe that there is a God, much less to sort out the details of how God might have created the universe and be relating to creation at present. An unknown writer in the fourteenth century, who believed in God, nevertheless thought that God was ultimately unknowable in an intellectual sense. He had only one suggestion of how God might be known. 'Of God himself no man can think. He may well be loved, but not thought. By love he may be grasped and held; by thought never.' The writer describes our lack of knowledge and understanding as a great, dark 'cloud of unknowing', and urges anyone who wants to know God to 'smite upon that thick cloud of unknowing with a sharp dart of longing love. Come what may, do not give up.'[3]

According to this man, the only way to understand God is to love him, and to persevere with this loving no matter what. But what about those who cannot say that they believe in, or love, God? Are we really any closer to the answers to questions like 'How can I know God exists?' and 'How can I know God loves me?' Is it possible that creation reveals truth about God, if only we could understand it?

The oft-controversial former Bishop of Edinburgh, Richard Holloway, in non-controversial mode describes an 'intuition of faith' that comes before any rational awareness. 'This great intuition is more difficult to talk about sensibly: it is an experience of presence, of meaning, but words alone cannot convey any sense of it.' He adds that some people find themselves 'invaded by meaning' in ways that lead to belief. 'Mysteries of recognition sometimes draw from us an exultant cry of faith.'[4] Has the capacity for faith and the ability to know God been built into our beings? This is important, because I believe that God has created us with the capacity for faith, and I also believe that God has revealed himself in creation. God may be shrouded in mystery, but God is not deliberately coy. The wonder that we are here at all should take us quite a way down the road of faith.

I expect, though, that it requires an element of faith even to talk about God, and for those who do not yet know God, there may be the sense of a strange restlessness or a fierce curiosity. It's probably best described as the mental, spiritual and emotional equivalent of being physically hungry, that strange but intense hunger when you don't quite know what it is that you want to eat. C. S. Lewis famously described a 'God-shaped hole' in each of us, which would remain empty until we knew God. But if the only real way to know God is to love him, and the only way to love God is to know him, where do we begin?

The simple answer is, we don't. *We* don't, but *God* does, or perhaps I should say did. Remember, 'In the beginning, *God* . . .'. Not us. We do not bear on our shoulders or in our souls the weight of being the ones who started it all. Life isn't something that we've done to ourselves. We didn't dream up the world around us, as some people have clearly regretted. To put it rather delicately, as did Alfonso the Wise way back in the thirteenth century, 'Had I been present at creation, I would have given some useful hints for the better ordering of the universe.' Those may be sentiments shared by many, but they don't change the fact that *we* weren't there. Life, the universe and everything is God's party, and he's invited us.

Our greatest mission in life, should we choose to accept it, is to respond to God's ongoing, never-ending invitation, which is extended to everyone. There aren't different types of invitations for different people. There aren't different parties. God is offering the same to everyone. If you're reading this, you've already accepted God's first gift, which is the gift of life. There's a lot more on offer, but let's first take a closer look at the God who has created this world that we inhabit.

### The God of risk

As I stray into some of the more complex and mysterious areas about the nature of the Creator of our universe, I would like to register my gratitude to John Polkinghorne, whom I have already mentioned. He has been my main guide in my quest to understand the kind of God revealed from the facts of the universe. I owe John another debt, as well.

From time to time throughout my life I have been seized by the unlovely sensations of claustrophobia. I can go for years without an attack, and I never know when it will strike. When I was a child, it happened occasionally when I was riding in the back of a two-door car, and once, unforgettably, as I was climbing up inside the Statue of Liberty. Mercifully, it vanished for ages, and I thought it had gone for good, but it suddenly reappeared when I was on a plane, flying home after my father's funeral.

A few days after that, I was on a train, travelling home from London. Without warning, the train stopped, and there we sat, with no indication of what had gone wrong or when we would be under way again. I could feel the rising dread, and I quickly grabbed John's book, *Science and Creation*, which I just happened to be reading, from my handbag. I buried myself in it, and read it, slowly and carefully. I didn't let myself move on from one sentence to the next until I was fairly certain that I had understood what he had written. I found the book so fascinating and so demanding that I was able to concentrate against my panic. In time, the train began to move, and for the rest of the journey I continued to absorb, albeit more happily, some of the most exciting and challenging thinking I'd ever read about the interplay between science and theology.

To kick off, Polkinghorne considers that for God to be the type of God defined by Christianity, God must be 'free'. God is not locked in some cosmic wrestling match with another comparable being, such as an antigod. God's will is not ultimately threatened by another equal but opposing force, such as the existence of antigod magic. Yet, 'the God who is eternally free is not an imperious dictator exercising an arbitrary will. He is *internally* constrained by the consistency of his own nature.'[5] But consistency doesn't mean mechanistic predictability. The old image of God as a 'divine Clockmaker' who wound up the universe at the beginning of time, only to sit back and watch it unwind, doesn't work any more. Now we perceive God more as a God of risk, who created a world that is 'at once more open to innovation in its process and more dangerously precarious in its possible outcome'.[6]

Perhaps it is only this type of world which can accommodate the existence of love. If love is freely given, and if it is to remain true to its nature, then there has to be built into our universe the element of risk, the risk that we might not love in return. If this is so, then a better image for God might be the 'divine Juggler', a God who still interacts with his creation, but whose Being leaves the possibility for chance. As anyone who has ever played Monopoly will know, chance can bring joy or disaster. The reality is that ours is a world in which cancer and other horrible diseases can occur, but God is not the one who gives us disease, although 'he is responsible for allowing the world to be such that it can happen'.[7]

The important thing is that the risk isn't all one-sided. It's not as if we, the creation, do all the suffering and pick up the tab for God's great idea of the necessity of free will. God also suffers and also takes part in the risk. The act of creating the type of world we live in would have involved a *kenosis* of God, which means an emptying out of God and 'an acceptance of the self-limitation inherent in the giving of creative love'.[8] It was a risk for God to become involved with an act of creation and required vulnerability, a quality not usually associated with the Divine! The almighty, conquering, triumphant king is a view of God at odds with the view of a risk-taking vulnerable lover, driven only by the longing and desire to love and be loved. If we put our faith in this God, we put our faith in God's continuing commitment to us and his never-ending love for us.

Perhaps this is the only way that love can work. Perhaps if it were more of a sure thing, with less chance of it all going wrong, we would be back to the Clockmaker, or, at the very least, to a Puppetmaster. As it is, I think that our risk-taking God has called us to accept, with him, the long and sometimes painful process that the work of love requires.

This thought of God, gradually working with and through creation towards the ultimate triumph of love, involves a theological concept called teleology. Teleology is to do with the bringing about of the *telos*, the perfect fulfilment of all of creation. This *telos* can be said to occur when the whole world has been brought back into a loving relationship with God.

It is not a case of pie-in-the-sky-by-and-by, where people get rewarded for their good works, but, basically, everything else in the world stays the same. Rather, the *telos* is the hope of a wholly renewed existence for all of creation, made possible by Jesus Christ, who will 'reconcile to himself all things, whether on earth or in heaven' (Colossians 1:20). This ultimate fulfilment is supposed to come about because God wills that it should be so, and God, being God, has the patience to wait for it.

Meanwhile, we walk a risky, uncertain path, looking forward to ultimate union with a God who loved us so much that he would only accept our freely given response. Union with this God will not result in our eventual annihilation or anonymity, but in intimate, dynamic, complete fulfilment. Our present existence on earth, which to allow for love has also to allow for suffering, is part of a greater whole which only God can fully envisage, but one in which we can know ourselves to be actively involved. Looked at this way, life takes on a somewhat different perspective!

## Down to earth

Butt let's just look at our own amazing planet! I get excited when I see the jackdaws grooming my Anglo-Nubian goats in the spring, taking as their payment small tufts of the goats' soft fluffy winter coat to line their nests. I get excited when these same goats stretch over the fence dividing them and their horse neighbours, so that they in turn can groom the horses! I like watching the fat green woodpecker that comes to hunt for grubs in our lawn. I could quite happily watch the 'nature' I know for hours on end. I've already spent what probably amounts to several years just staring at the sea, and I must say I feel the better for it!

My aunt, Eudoxia Woodward, has spent the last 25 years studying the mathematical designs of nature, in particular the geometry of plants and flowers. As a painter, she has enjoyed exploring (and painting) phenomena such as the Fibonacci series, a naturally occurring sequence that can be seen in sunflower seed heads and on pine cones and pineapples.

In his many television series, David Attenborough has opened up the amazing reality of our natural world to millions of people who would otherwise have never been able to see it. Before him, Jacques Cousteau introduced a whole generation of viewers to the wonder of life in the oceans.

Our explorations continue, but there is still so much we don't know about the meaning of life. If only we could be genuinely satisfied that the answer was 42, as helpfully suggested in *The Hitchhiker's Guide to the Galaxy*! It seems that the more we learn, the more we discover that there is more to learn! And so it goes. Discovery leading to new information, leading to new knowledge, leading to new discovery, ad infinitum.

For instance, astronomers are now saying that because of the time available for light to travel since the Big Bang, we can set the present boundaries of our universe at a distance of about 15 billion light years. As time carries on we can expect to be able to see even further into the universe, and who knows how much bigger we shall discover it to be.

With such a vast universe, is it statistically likely that life exists somewhere else other than on planet Earth? If so, in what form, and how could we ever find out? How can we explain the incredibly delicate balance of the building blocks of our universe, such as the force of gravity or the velocity of light? If either of these had been slightly different, life would not and could not have developed as it did.

The Earth is tilted at an angle of 23 degrees to its orbit, which produces our seasons. If the Earth were not tilted just so, vapours from the oceans would have moved both north and south, resulting in inhabitable continents of ice. Evidently, if the moon were only 50,000 miles away from Earth, instead of 200,000, the tides would be so huge that all the continents would be under water.

If the oceans had been a few feet deeper, carbon dioxide and oxygen would have been absorbed, and no life would exist. If the Earth's crust had been a few feet thicker, there would also be no oxygen – and no life. If ice were more dense than water in its liquid state then the world would be totally barren, because ice is not a good conductor of heat, and it would never melt.[9] If ... if ... the mind boggles! How did our universe get it right? How is it possible that we exist in the way we do, with air to breathe, water to drink and food to eat?

The fact that we exist at all, the fact that you and I live on a whirling bit of stone and fire we call planet Earth, and don't fall off or get dizzy, seems to me entirely improbable and completely amazing. I confess with a wild sort of glee, that there is so much I don't understand, that *all* of life seems like a mystery and a miracle. To be sure, some of the things that we humans have invented are very clever, but they pale into insignificance compared to the world around us. Designing a huge ship made of steel and concrete that can float on the surface of the ocean is exceedingly clever. But think about the ocean itself. Now that's really clever!

In this chapter I've offered a few thoughts about life, the universe, our own incredible planet, and the Creator who made it all possible. Now let's look more closely into the nature of the One who is magnificent and mysterious, and yet able to be known through the giving and receiving of love.

## 2

## Partners in the Dance

### Who is God?

If grappling with the complexities of a universe we can see is intellectually stretching, then how do we cope with trying to look more closely at God, whom we cannot see? I've hinted at some of the characteristics of God the Creator, but most Christians worship a God who is more than 'just' Creator. We also say that we believe in a God who provides for us, who has made certain promises to us, and who is always present with us.

A few months ago when I was travelling by train to York, a small elderly man who had got on the train at Doncaster came over and started talking to me. His Yorkshire accent was so broad that at first I could hardly understand him. He was gripping a rolled-up copy of *Racing Times*, and so I deduced that he was headed for the races, scheduled to take place in York later in the day.

Sure enough, he told me how he was a betting man, and how he loved coming to the races. I asked him whether he could pick the winners, and he smiled and said that, over a season, he never lost any money but he never came out too far ahead, either.

He then asked me what I was reading. It happened to be a background paper on some theological issue, which I was reading in preparation for a summer session of the General Synod, the Church of England's legislative body. I explained this to him, expecting a sharp exit on his part. However, this man's eyes brightened and he seemed to be genuinely interested. From then on, we talked about God and, particularly, whether it was possible to know God. He was clearly a believer, and yet he seemed hesitant about something.

All of a sudden he said, 'I get strange thoughts.' I asked him in what way were they strange. He then told me about how he would occasionally get premonitions, or know with great certainty which horse to bet on. We talked about the extraordinary capacity of the human mind, and about the spiritual dimension to reality.

He paused for a moment and then told me about an experience he had had almost fifteen years earlier. He had been in a large room in a hotel, taking part in a game of bingo. It was a happy, lively event, involving about four hundred people. He described how at one point he was looking out over the vast room, idly watching everyone laughing and talking, when he became aware that he could hear and understand what everyone in the room was saying. He sat frozen while what was happening slowly sank in: four hundred people all chatting to their friends, and he could hear and make sense of each conversation distinctly, and at the same time. Suddenly, he became frightened. What was happening? As his fear swept over him, the experience faded, and once again he was just one man in a noisy room.

'I didn't know what to do about it,' he told me, obviously distressed, 'I didn't know what it meant. I was so frightened. I just blocked myself off and tried to pretend it had never happened.' As we talked about his extraordinary experience, it came to me that he was describing what I believed about God's capability to listen to all people who were reaching out and calling for help, or saying thank you, or just responding to God's love for them. What had happened to him, I suggested, might be an indication of the way God's mind works.

I told the man that I did not think that he should be afraid of what had happened, and that it seemed to me that he had had a glimpse of an aspect of what it was like to think like Christ. I also told him that I thought such experiences were usually given to help others, to encourage people. He said that he knew he had gifts, but that he thought it was now too late. By blocking himself off from them, he reckoned that God had given up on him. I asked him whether he would be willing from now on to use his gifts for God's purposes. He said he was willing, but wondered whether, as he was in his seventies, he was too old. In the few minutes that remained before the train pulled into York station, I tried to reassure him that with God it was never too late. If he was willing, God was more than willing, and that he must try to trust that God still wanted to relate to him. He then helped me off with my bags and walked me to the taxi rank. When he left, he gripped my hands in his. I told him my name and said that I would pray for him. He told me that his name was George, and he thanked me.

I was absolutely astounded by our meeting. Never before had I heard of anyone who had experienced such a phenomenon. I have thought a lot about it, but still the best explanation I have is that, for a brief moment, George was given an insight into an ability, or characteristic, that I have always assumed God has. I have always taken it for granted that God can hear all of us at the same time. Why should I be so surprised if some people are occasionally given a similar ability? Also, if it is true that we humans only use about one-tenth of the capacity of our brains, perhaps such experiences might be more possible than we think. Perhaps George's experience is but a small glimpse of the potential we all share. Perhaps there is a lot more to being made in the image of God than we can possibly imagine.

## Getting hold of God

We look to God for meaning and purpose in our lives. Above all, we say that God is love. John V. Taylor, the former Bishop of Winchester, was convinced that the only power of 'Almighty' God is the power of love, a love that is vulnerable and suffers with us.

The Nicene Creed, the statement of faith agreed at the Council of Nicaea in the fourth century, and which is still held to be the best summary of the Christian faith, identifies three Beings, three Persons as part of God: God the Father, God the Son and God the Holy Spirit. Seeing God as Three in One, the Trinity, has helped us to understand God, but it's not as if we are worshipping three different gods; that would be polytheism. It's more as if we are trying to get hold of as much as we can of the truth about God.

In the fable about the blind men and the elephant, the first blind man grabbed hold of the elephant's trunk and announced that an elephant is like a snake. The second man felt the elephant's leg, and declared that an elephant is like a tree. The third caught hold of the elephant's tail, and exclaimed that an elephant is like a rope. The fourth leaned against the elephant's side, and swore that the elephant is like a wall. Who was right?

They were, of course, all right, and yet their partial understandings about the elephant did not add up to the whole truth about the elephant. In fact, their individual perceptions did not even add up to a realistic description of an elephant. In a way, that could be said to be like theology: blind men telling each other about the bit of the elephant that they have got hold of, and making suppositions about the rest of the elephant.

It's awfully difficult to describe the whole truth about God. Some descriptions might be more true or accurate than others, but all descriptions are incomplete. The truth of God is always greater than what we can say about God. If anyone tries to tell you that they have got God all sewn up and neatly packaged, don't believe them. God is infinite, as love is infinite.

## God as Three in One

I've already mentioned the Trinity, which is an understanding of God that was developed largely from some of the things that Jesus said about himself and his relationship with his heavenly Father, and about the Holy Spirit. Jesus repeatedly claimed that he had been sent, and that he had a special relationship with the One who had sent him. He told his disciples, 'Who ever believes in me believes not in me but in him who sent me . . . for I have not spoken on my own, but the Father who sent me has himself given me a commandment about what to say and what to speak' (John 12:44, 49).

Jesus says to Thomas, one of his disciples, 'I am the way, and the truth and the life. No one comes to the Father except through me. If you had known me, you would have known my Father also' (John 14:6–7). Philip, another disciple, then asks Jesus to show them the Father. Jesus replies, 'Have I been with you so long and you still do not know me, Philip? Whoever has seen me has seen the Father' (John 14:9). Jesus goes on to say that his Father will send the Holy Spirit to teach the disciples all truth and to remind them of what Jesus has taught them. At the beginning of Acts, Luke quotes Jesus telling the disciples that 'John baptised with water, but you will be baptised with the Holy Spirit not many days from now' (Acts 1:5).

In the letters that Paul wrote, he freely distinguished between God, Jesus Christ and the Holy Spirit. He frequently opened his letters with the greeting, 'Grace and peace from God our Father and the Lord Jesus Christ' (Romans 1:7; 1 Corinthians 1:3; 2 Corinthians 1:2; Galatians 1:3; etc.), and signed off with similar words. His closing words in 2 Corinthians have been used to form what is now called 'the grace': 'The grace of our Lord Jesus Christ and the love of God and the fellowship of the Holy Spirit be with us all evermore.'

Understandings of the Trinity have changed over the years. At various times in history (and perhaps there are still those who see it this way) the Trinity has been thought to imply a hierarchy of importance, with the Father being the senior partner, the Son coming next in line, followed by the Holy Spirit, the junior member of the partnership. However, in the fourth century three theologians got together (a Basil and two Gregorys) and decided that there could not be any hierarchy in the Trinity.

Instead, the three Persons of the Trinity were to be seen as separate and distinct, but also interdependent and equal. They live in one another and are part of each other, but they still have individual identities. Their continual give and take of love creates an internal dynamic unity, a communion of the Three in One.

The early theologians called this state of the internal relationship of the Divine *perichoresis,* and trying to describe the exact nature of what it means is even more difficult than the blind men trying to describe an elephant! One of the most important things about *perichoresis* is that it implies that the three Persons of the Trinity exist as separate persons *only in relation to each other.* The Father is only the Father because of the Son, and likewise the Son is only the Son in relation to the Father. There is no Father-like Being all on his own, nor any Son-like Being all on his own: both Beings are the way they are only in relation to the other. The Spirit, also, is a full member of the Godhead, and shares the same relationship with the other two Persons of the Trinity as they share with the Spirit. Because the Spirit has not been called by the names of identifiable persons in any human relationships, it makes it easier to grasp the Spirit's divine nature. (Perhaps that makes it more difficult for some, but at least it avoids the obvious human parallels, which, inevitably, mislead.)

One early writer, Bernard of Clairvaux, spoke about the Holy Spirit as the never-ending kiss between the Father and the Son. Others have used the imagery of perfume to describe the Trinity. There is the bottle, the liquid and the scent that floats on the air and fills the room; all aspects are needed in order to have perfume. Yet other writers have chosen the analogy of sunlight reflected off the surface of water onto a white wall. The dancing shapes on the wall would not be possible without the water, the sunlight and the wall.

One of my own homespun analogies is that of a plait of hair. Each of the three locks is distinct, and when woven together they make something that is like each of the locks separately, but also different. The plait is made of one head of hair, but it could not exist as it does without the three distinct parts. By far the biggest problem with this analogy is that it fails to capture the way in which each of the separate, but interrelated, Beings of the Trinity *indwell* each other. In fact, for some it is the ongoing *dynamic* of God that is most important, and they even suggest it is more accurate to describe God as a verb instead of a noun – any noun. For others, God is *Being* itself, not a definable Being; again a difficult concept to pin down with words.

But most theologians *do* see the nature and main characteristic of the trinitarian God as a continual interchange of love. Because this love is not static, it has often been said that the three Persons of the Trinity exist in a perpetual dance of love. This is seen as a dance in which the three dancers take part equally. There are no leaders and no followers, but all three in turn initiate and respond to one another's movements, and, together, they create the dance.

When a person responds to the love of God, they are caught up and become partners in this Divine Dance. In fact, to call God the Divine Dance of Never-Ending Love is probably as apt a name as any, only with one major problem: it fails to convey the Person-ness of God.

However, we need to remind ourselves continually that when we speak about God, the names we use can only ever hint at, but never fully describe, the truth. Thomas Aquinas, writing back in the thirteenth century, considered that only abstract nouns should be used to describe God. So, for instance, Aquinas believed that it was true to say that God is love, but that to call God 'Father', or 'the Almighty', or any other non-abstract noun, was to paint a partial, and therefore not entirely accurate, picture of God. What stands out most for me is that the common thread that runs through centuries of people attempting to define and describe God is the description of God as love.

The idea of understanding God through love has been around for a long, long time. But more than that, we are invited to discover that

God is Love. We are not meant merely to gaze on the Godhead and wonder wistfully what it would be like to be involved in that type of relationship. God's intention for us is to leap in and join in the dance, and the more the merrier!

The image of the dance captures the *aliveness* of God, and the possibility that we can relate to God. If someone were to go through his or her entire life thinking about God, reading about God and talking about God, there would still be something missing. That's why the best we can do to describe what it's like to experience God is to describe an intimate, loving relationship. God is always trying to draw others in to become partners in the dance. In a way, it doesn't even make sense to talk about God without also talking about being in a relationship with God. I have said before that Love is an abstract name we give God to best describe who God is, but love can never be experienced in an abstract way. Like a kiss, love requires involvement, action and relationship.

### The person of Jesus Christ

The gospel of John opens with one of the most magnificent passages ever written:

> In the beginning was the Word, and the Word was with God, and the Word was God. He was in the beginning with God; all things were made through him, and without him was not anything made that was made. In him was life, and the life was the light of men. The light shines in the darkness, and the darkness has not overcome it. (John 1:1–5)

In the first few verses the gospel-writer sketches a new type of creation story, focusing not on the beginning of the world but on the coming of the 'Word', a term used for the person of Jesus Christ. The book of Genesis tells how God created the heavens and the earth, water, dry land, the sun, moon and stars, animals, and so on, ending with the creation of humans. Here, at the beginning of John's gospel, we read of the activity of the Word. Who or what is this Word that has co-existed with God and that corresponds to God?

In verse 14 John states, 'And the Word became flesh and dwelt among us . . .' and by the end of the opening passage he names Jesus

Christ as the bearer of grace and truth, and calls him the 'only Son' of the Father. It seems that he intends the reader to draw the conclusion that Jesus Christ is the Son of God, the Word about whom he has written. The message underlying the words is that the God who made us and all of creation, the God who has always existed, has now entered our world as the man Jesus. This act of God entering our world as a human is called the incarnation, and it 'testifies to God's deepest possible involvement with his creation'.[1]

I find it peculiar that the opening chapter of the gospel that goes on to speak of the love of God perhaps more eloquently and powerfully than anywhere else in the New Testament should have no mention of the word 'love'. By chapter 3 we have the famous assertion, 'For God so loved the world that he gave his only Son, that whoever believes in him should not perish but have eternal life.' The first chapter does not mention love, but speaks instead of light and darkness, grace and truth. Yet those opening verses of John describe in cosmic and spiritual terms the coming to earth of the One who revealed to us, above all else, God's love for us and identification with us.

When we look at Jesus we see a perfect image of the invisible God. In Jesus we also get a glimpse of how God wants us to be; Jesus is God's idea of what it is to be fully human. He shows not only what the divine nature is, but also what the perfect human nature can be. My psychotherapist friend Karina has said to me again and again that Jesus came to remind us of who we are and of who God is. She thinks the main problem with humanity is that we have forgotten who we are, how much like Christ we are really meant to be. Some of us may see that more clearly than others, but we have all, in varying degrees, forgotten our divine inheritance. We have given up on the possibility of peace, because we have forgotten that we bring the peace of God wherever we go. We have grown weary of helping others, because we have forgotten that we have the power within us to heal and give hope. We have colluded with the necessity of arms and warfare, because we have forgotten that love is the greatest power there is.

The incarnation, the coming of Jesus into our world at a special time in history, shows us in a way that nothing else possibly can, that it is freely given love, love that longs to give as well as to receive, that characterises the God who made us. This love, and this relationship, hints at the deepest meaning and purpose to our lives. The person of Jesus lived as we *can*, and loved as God *is*. What empowered and inspired Jesus can empower and inspire us, because he was filled then, as we can be now, with the Spirit of God.

Once we accept that Jesus is God, there can be no part of our understanding of God that would exclude what Jesus did in his earthly existence. Jesus, as both God and human, spent the final years of his earthly life ministering to people, touching and healing them, showing them what the kingdom of God was like, trying to give them the hope and vision of what they and life could be like if they lived in the light of what he said and did.

I suppose Jesus is the only person who has ever lived who was never tempted to say, 'Do as I say, not as I do', because Jesus' actions were entirely consistent with what he said. That is a goal which some of us may have, but which none of us can live up to perfectly. There will always be times when something we do or say, or think, will make hypocrites of us.

But Jesus didn't only teach and heal, he also endured great suffering and died an agonising death. In the light of the whole of Jesus' life, we are driven to an understanding of God as One who, unlike the uninvolved Clockmaker, and even going further than the risk-taking Juggler, shares in our sufferings. Dietrich Bonhoeffer, the German Lutheran pastor who was hanged for his part in an attempt to murder Hitler, was convinced that God suffered with the world through Jesus. Bonhoeffer was so conscious of God's suffering that he regarded his own suffering as insignificant. He wrote that 'to be a Christian means participating in the suffering of God in the life of the world. Only a suffering God can help.'[2]

John Austin Baker, the former Bishop of Salisbury, puts this view of God succinctly when he states that the 'crucified Jesus is the only accurate picture of God the world has ever seen'.[3] Any understanding of God that ignores the life and death of Jesus ignores the clearest picture we have of God. That is what the fuss over Jesus is all about. His story is not just about a good man, driven to a hideous and early death, but the actual involvement of God in our experience of life. And Jesus wasn't significant only for the brief time that he lived on earth: what he did has changed everything for all people for all time. Many believe that 'the presence of Jesus in history was the presence of God as he has always been and always will be.'[4] The writer of Hebrews describes Jesus as 'the same yesterday and today and for ever' (Hebrews 13:8). Whoever he was when he walked on Earth, he is still.

Furthermore, whatever Jesus accomplished on the cross, its effect was not time-limited; it was a once-and-for-all event, with its ripples extending into eternity. This is why, although every human being still sins, still falls short of what we know we can be, we do not have to pay the fine, if you like, for all the wrong we have done and will do. We will suffer, because that is the nature of this imperfect world and our imperfect natures, and a consequence of a world in which freely given love is possible, but we can accept the way God sees us now. Because of Jesus, we are perfectly loveable.

Jesus, who became the Christ, is the God who lived in flesh and blood as one of us, and yet who never lost his vision of who he could be. Perhaps I should say that this was the God who grew to understand that he was God! I doubt very much that as a baby and little child Jesus had the vision of who he was. The first signs of any special self-awareness are when he was about twelve, when he stayed behind in the Temple in Jerusalem, after his parents had already left for home. When they finally found him, three days later, his rather cryptic, cheeky-sounding explanation was that he had stayed in the Temple because he 'must be in my Father's house'. I can imagine how that went down with Joseph! It certainly caused Mary to ponder. What Jesus had been doing was sitting with the teachers, listening and asking questions. Evidently, they had all been amazed at the perception and understanding of this young boy.

Because of Jesus, God offers us the gift of grace, which is a new way of being and living. We don't have to, indeed, we can't, earn it or deserve it. It is God's free gift to us, free because of the way Jesus lived and died. To live in God's grace is to accept what Jesus did for us, and to accept that we can never earn our own halos, we can never save ourselves. Grace is Jesus stepping in for us, wiping out our sin, and throwing a party for us. Grace is the love of Christ going to the limit for us.

I don't mean to be irreverent, but sometimes I like to see the time from when Jesus was taken off the cross and buried to the time he rose again rather like a flat green lawn, with love as the burrowing mole. For the time Jesus was dead, the lawn remained smooth and even, but all the while, unseen by anyone, love was at work, and on the third day, love exploded, like a mole surfacing in a mountain of earth! Love had never stopped, it's just that no one could see it working. God's love had kept on through the suffering, through all the pain and hatred, through even physical death, and when it re-emerged it changed a disaster into a triumph.

When the world had thrown its worst at Jesus, Jesus took it, still believing more in the love he shared with his Father, trusting to the end that God's love was greater than anything else, even death. Jesus' faith in his heavenly Father, his loyalty, obedience and endurance, were all based on his belief that God's love was the only way; the purpose and the reason, the *why* and the *how* and the *what* of all of life.

There is nothing else that God has, or that God is, that can do more. When we talk about an omnipotent God, we are not imply-ing a power to control, but precisely the opposite. We mean a power that loves enough to give us a chance to love back. There is noth-ing in the universe that can cause God's love to falter, fail or fall, and Jesus showed us what life could be like, lived under the influence of love.

Jesus trusted in God in a way that no one else had ever trusted, and his trust gave love a chance to show what it was capable of doing. Yet even Jesus, like us, had at some point to take a step of faith. If Jesus had known for sure that God would be there, waiting to bring him back to new life after death, there would have been no risk involved, and therefore no trust required. On the cross when Jesus cried, 'Why have you left me?' he was stepping out into the dark abyss, not knowing if God was there, not knowing what was to become of him.

If only we could see that this universe was made to run on love, that love is not a sentimental option for a few idealists, but the sum of what we need to live as we were created to live. It is up to us to open ourselves to God's love, or we will end up fighting it and try-ing to make do with something else. All the other ways of reaching our goals can only go so far. Only love, only this love-in-relation-ship with God will never let us down, even though it is not the easy option. Choosing love took Jesus to the cross, but it also led to the resurrection, and after the resurrection Jesus started preparing his friends for a whole new way of life, which brings us to the third Person of the Trinity, the Holy Spirit.

## The Holy Spirit

God never intended us to read about Jesus, sigh, shrug and say, 'Oh, well, it's all right for him; he was really God.' I think God intended us to look hard at what Jesus said and did, and say, 'Wow! So that's what it's all about. That's who Christ is, that's the way I can be.' Jesus made possible, and also showed us, the way we can become all that we were created to be, which is like him, and he did so through the power of God's Spirit.

After Jesus had been raised from the dead, and before he went up to heaven, he made certain promises to his friends. One of the things he promised was that the Holy Spirit would come and teach the disciples all they need to know and remind them of what Jesus had told them (John 14:26). Jesus also told them that the Spirit would convince the world concerning sin and righteousness (John 16:8). Together, the Father, Jesus and the Spirit would come and live in those who love God and who keep God's commandments (John 14:23).

The overarching message that Jesus was trying to convey about the Spirit is one of help, wisdom, discernment and power. Time and again Jesus also breathed the promise and blessing of peace: 'Peace I leave with you; my peace I give to you; not as the world gives do I give to you. Let not your hearts be troubled, neither let them be afraid' (John 14:27). Jesus is trying to tell his close friends in as many ways as possible that, although he is leaving, they will not be bereft. In fact, Jesus hints that if only they understood, they would rejoice at what was going to happen to him and at the new relationship they themselves would soon be experiencing.

With this type of build-up, it is easy to see why the disciples were looking forward to, and yet were confused about, a supposedly new relationship with the Holy Spirit. They did as Jesus asked, and gathered in a room together, waiting for the promise to be fulfilled about the coming of the Holy Spirit. They had no idea what would happen, and they were certainly in for a shock!

Instead of a human replacement for Jesus, who might have been expected to knock gently on the door and ask politely to come in, Jesus' friends were nearly blown away by what started as a wild wind and then turned into flames of fire that crackled above their heads. Along with these pyrotechnics was an uncontrollable urge to pour out their hearts to God in completely unknown languages.

When they stumbled out of the room and into the streets of Jerusalem, still praising God, not surprisingly some people thought they were drunk. But Peter managed to convince the milling crowds that they hadn't touched a drop, but that God had touched them! That first day of the Spirit coming, following a passionate sermon by Peter, about three thousand people repented of their sins and asked to be baptised in the name of Jesus Christ.

From then on the disciples were on fire, not with little flames above their heads but with a huge fire burning inside them. They began to carry on the ministry that Jesus had begun, as Jesus had told them they would, and which they hadn't believed was possible. They healed people, cast out demons, and preached and taught with great authority. They organised a new way of living, and pooled resources so that they had enough to care for the poor. It was pretty obvious that these men and women were different, and the difference was the Holy Spirit.

One of the most exciting and amazing aspects of being a Christian is that we believe that the Spirit who comes to us today is the same Spirit that came to the disciples all those years ago. However, I have met people who are fairly happy with the idea of God and who can cope with the thought of Jesus, but who are terrified of the Holy Spirit! They keep God at arm's length because they are so worried that they will take the step of faith, only to find themselves tearing around the place holding open-air rallies and jabbering unintelligibly. They forget that the Spirit of God is the One who fills us and helps us to be like Christ.

Only by opening ourselves to the Holy Spirit can we come to know God deeply and intimately, in a way that is beyond 'head' knowledge. It is the Holy Spirit who revitalises our own spirits and who breathes into us the wisdom, will and power to live as Jesus lived. We will never attain perfection, but, thanks to God's Spirit, we will be able to join in the dance, and take our places as members of the Body of Christ. As Paul says, 'we are to grow up in every way like Christ, who is the head of his body, the Church. Under his direction the whole body is fitted together perfectly, and each part in its own special way helps the other parts, so that the whole body is healthy and growing and full of love' (Ephesians 4:15–16).

## A new relationship

One of the things I have learned over the years is that God has no favourites. Everyone can form a relationship with God, but God does not prefer certain people to others. When we come to God, we come as little children, that is, open and receptive to a parent's love. The emphasis is on God choosing us, making us his children. The apostle John writes that those who believe in God are given the right to become God's children (John 1:12). In many of his letters, Paul uses the concept of adoption to try to describe this relationship we have with God.

> At the heart of adoption lie both a longing and a promise: there is a child needing, we assume, to be somebody's child; and a prospective parent, someone with, for whatever reason, a space in their living and loving that has yet to be occupied. And out of that meeting of longings comes a promise that creates the relationship that previously did not exist. It is a relationship newly created, that does not depend on the sharing of a past, as blood ties do; for there is no shared past. It depends on the possibility and hope of a shared future.[5]

Jesus succinctly describes this new type of relationship for those who seek God. At one point, he is preaching to a large group of people crammed into a house. Someone tells him that his mother and brothers are outside wanting to see him, and that they can't get in because of the crowd of people. Jesus answers, 'My mother and brothers are those who hear the word of God and do it' (Luke 8:21). For me, this is one of the most radical comments of Jesus ever recorded. At a stroke, Jesus seemingly makes null and void all blood ties, and instead states that the only ties he recognises are those based on obedience to God. If I were his mother I would have felt extremely hurt and offended. If I were his sibling I would have been outraged. How dare Jesus ignore his family? How dare he dismiss his biological roots? But perhaps Jesus wasn't dismissing his biological roots, in order to be rude to his family. Perhaps he was more concerned to emphasise the importance of the new relationship that exists for those who follow God.

Many people come from happy, loving families, but many others come from families where the fact of being related to each other is a heavy burden. Clearly Jesus loved and respected his mother; remember how he made sure she would be looked after by his friend John, when he was gone. But his message to his disciples in that crowded house was the promise of a new type of 'family' based on the (paradoxically) liberating obedience to God, rather than on any human ties or connections. This means that no matter how I came into being, what family I was raised in, what I was told about who I was, or wasn't, my true spiritual identity is as part of the Body of Christ.

Such a new identity cuts two ways. For those who would dearly love to escape from negative painful family relations, it is a message of liberation and hope. For those who rely on their good family name and standing to give them their identity, it is a reminder that God looks at the heart and spirit, not at your last name, home address, or what you or your parents do for a living. In this new 'family' what counts is how we respond to God, how open our hearts and spirits are to the One who offers us new life. Beauty, brains, wealth and social status, or the lack of them, neither hinder nor help us to enter into this new relationship. They are simply not part of the criteria for belonging. What matters is how we respond to God.

One of the things many people have to face is that God is God, and not your daddy or your mummy. Your parents are hurting children too, even if they hurt you. It might be helpful to examine what they and other significant adults taught us about God, and ourselves, and decide whether it is consistent with what we now believe. As the old saying goes, God doesn't have any grandchildren. At some point, each of us has to start responding to God for ourselves.

Growing up in God is very much to do with accepting God's view of who I am, who you are, and who God is. It is taking steps in faith on our own, without always having to hold someone else's hand. It is taking responsibility for what we believe and what we do with what we believe.

If you don't think God intends for people to live in poverty, what are you doing about it? If you think that part of being a child of God is meeting together with other believers, what are you doing about it? If you believe that Christians should never allow themselves to become boring and pompous and stuffy, how are you ensuring that you never become any of these things? If your idea of maturity includes staying open to the wonder of the world around us, and able to respond with a fair amount of spontaneity to the people and opportunities we encounter in life, how are you taking care to grow to this type of maturity? How can we learn to treat life and ourselves and others as precious, while at the same time sit lightly to our status and achievements?

I believe that there is a divine paradox at the heart of growing up: the more 'mature' we get as followers of Christ, the more child-like we become. The less we will think we know it all, and the more we will realise that we are just beginners on this journey called life and the way called love. The less it will matter that we get life 'right', while, paradoxically, the more it will matter that we listen closely to God and heed the lightest breath of the Spirit. Like children, we will delight in play and laughter, we will take the risk of opening our hearts and lives and arms to the people we encounter, and we will reach out to those who are dying with the longing to be shown some sign that they are loved. We will extend the generous welcome of Christ, knowing that we have also been welcomed in the extravagance of God's love. We will look for ways of enjoying life, and bringing that joy to others, instead of ways of organising life and controlling others. We will create more 'free' time, where we will face the possibility that we will hear the voice of God, or the cries of others, or even the deep desires of our own hearts. We will risk curling up in the lap of God and forgetting our fears, knowing them to be but deceptive shadows. We will throw back our heads and laugh at the future, knowing it and ourselves to be held by the One who is the same yesterday, today and tomorrow.

## God beyond words

I started this chapter by trying to define God. I'm afraid a single, tidy definition still eludes me. I keep on coming back to an understanding of God as a dynamic Being, alive in an endless dance of love, in which we are all invited to participate. I expect I will always like thinking about who God is, and finding different ways of talking about God.

I would like to include a word about how we address God, which of course affects how we think about God. Although I sometimes call God my loving heavenly Father, and picture a Being who envelopes me with total, non-judging, all-accepting love, I also try to find images for God that help to avoid the trap of seeing God as a super-spiritualised male deity.

I'm afraid that for the purpose of writing this book, I have opted for the traditional use of the masculine pronoun when describing God. However, Christian doctrine tells us that God is neither male nor female, but that as our Creator, God encompasses both masculinity and femininity. Therefore, it is right to speak of God as having masculine or feminine attributes, but wrong to speak of God as being either male or female. God is properly neither a 'he' nor a 'she', but so far we have not come up with any successful alternatives. The closest I have seen is the use of S/he, but this, alas, still startles so many people that I have, with some regret, felt it was most appropriate in this case to follow tradition.

Personal pronouns may cause problems, but it is generally agreed that God can rightly be seen as both our Mother and Father. After one of her prophetic visions, Mother Julian wrote as if recording a message from God. In it she uses a great variety of images:

> It is I, the strength and goodness of fatherhood. It is I, the wisdom of motherhood. It is I, the light and grace of holy love. It is I, the Trinity, it is I, the unity. I am the sovereign goodness in all things. It is I who teach you to love. It is I who teach you to desire. It is I who am the reward of all true desiring.[6]

If she heard God correctly, then God seems to be quite relaxed about finding new ways of describing the Godself!

I think the important thing to stress is that God is personal, not an 'it' but a Person. In Jesus' day, the image of an intimate loving father, a daddy, spoke volumes to his listeners about someone who would not lord it over them, but who would reach out in love and compassion, someone who could do what they said they would do, someone entirely trustworthy. Jesus also used many different images for himself, such as the good shepherd, the vine, the door, bread, light, living water, even a reference to a mother hen.

It is also instructive to look at the qualities and characteristics that Jesus possessed, things such as kindness, compassion, gentleness, goodness and wisdom. In his dealings with people Jesus never treated anyone differently on the basis of their sex, and he made clear that the message of salvation and the way of discipleship was for everyone, both men and women.

Sadly, I think our adherence to exclusively masculine names and pronouns for God has affected our understanding of God. In fact, I think it has skewed and distorted our views of God, and the really difficult thing is, we can't be sure in what ways our views have been distorted. I believe we now have to work at discovering a God who has never preferred men for being male, and never held women at arm's length or considered them to be of less value because they were female. Remember Paul's great statement of liberation: 'In Christ there is neither Jew nor Greek, there is neither slave nor free, there is neither male nor female; for you are all one in Christ Jesus' (Galatians 3:28). Finding new appropriate ways of talking about God is one of the challenges that still faces us. I am confident that if we trust and listen, and maybe even take risks and experiment a bit, our gracious and loving God will shed light for the way ahead.

I will end with this poem written by a friend, the poet and journalist Martin Wroe, who offers his own answer to the question, who is God?

> god is
> where you are when you're at the end of your self
> god is
> who you are with when you are with no-one at all
> god is
> that feeling you have when you know your feelings can't
> be trusted
> god is
> underneath everything, above, not beyond
> and
> sometimes
> just by the side, leaning across, waiting for an invite
> god is
> behind the scenes, shuffling
> in the front row, laughing
> god is
> the fear of the known,

and the love of the unknown
god is
a hook to sling your awe on
a peg to hang out your adoration
god is
the who
who fills your heart when it's about to burst
god is
your mailbox, new message waiting
god is
what you don't have to say
when only your heart can say it
god is
inside the inside of in
and just out of reach, standing on tip toe
god is
what is before is comes into being
god is
what's left after all
god is
the sight of the place you knew you were after
god is
your first prayer
and your last resort
your blind suckling, your desperate striving,
your reluctant surrender, your dying breath
god is
who we hope for when all our hope has run out
god is
how to be
when we've finally done doing
god is
your hope
when you're down to your last four letters
your love
when you've got none left at all

## 3

# *Who Am I?*

I have seen people in Cambridge, which is just up the road from where I live, wearing T-shirts that proclaim, 'I'm not a tourist. I live here.' I know how they feel! Sometimes when I am shopping in Cambridge, I get asked by shop assistants, 'How long are you here for?' Immediately I am shaken out of my thoughts about what I am buying, or my next errand, and I realise that to the person behind the counter I am a stranger, and not just a stranger but a foreigner.

In answer to their question, I usually try to make a joke about being married to one of the 'natives', and being here 'for the duration'. I also get asked a lot, 'Where are you from?' Where indeed? For most of the nearly twenty-seven years I have been in England, I have lived in a small village in Hertfordshire, and yet I know that is not the answer that these questioners want. They want to know what makes me different, why my accent isn't like theirs, and, possibly, what I am doing here.

At times these small incidents catch me unawares, and I become self-conscious and am reminded that I am still in some ways an outsider. I have travelled so much and lived in so many different places that I find it unsatisfactory simply to say that I am 'from' America. Anyway, how do I know what images are springing into their minds when I say that? Are they picturing Las Vegas or Miami? I am aware that most people, even most Americans, cannot picture where I am from on Long Island. When I say 'Long Island' they might, at best, have a hazy view of an over-spill from New York City. Most people have no idea that the island is nearly one hundred miles long, and changes character drastically several times the further from Manahattan one travels. I have to explain that I was born in a small leafy town called Huntington, and then later on went to live in my grandparent's home out in the Hamptons, an area first settled by Native Americans who farmed and fished and lived peaceably. Much later, in the seventeenth century, the English came, bringing their place names, their plants and their customs, and, for many years now, arty New Yorkers flock to the Hamptons every summer, or, increasingly, stay all year round.

But even that doesn't explain that although I was born in America, and spent the first few years of my life there, I also lived on a boat and sailed in the West Indies and Europe. Do I bother to mention that I went to college in California, and that I have also lived in Virginia and in Illinois? Of course, for most of these encounters, a brief answer suffices, and I go on my way. Yet the questions I am asked sometimes get to the heart of what I think about myself and how I define myself.

I say I believe in a Creator of the universe. I find the concept of the Trinity helpful and true of my experience of God. On most days I see myself as a willing and joyous partner in the Divine Dance of Love, but it has taken a long time for me to be able to answer the simple question, 'Who am I?'

Perhaps it is because I have had to make so many changes, and because I have had to 'be myself' in so many different places, that I have thought long and hard about the question of identity. What is it that makes us who we are? Is our identity essentially tied up in where we are from, or in our families or our work – or what?

Shortly after my husband Chris and I moved to our first home, I went through times of feeling very much stripped to the bone. I don't know how better to describe it. A few months earlier I had been a single postgraduate student in America, with a large network of friends and family. All of a sudden, it seemed to me, I was a married woman with a husband I hardly knew, setting up home in an unfamiliar place, with no job and no friends. What is more, I was pregnant – an entirely new experience in itself.

Chris, who is English, and I had met in Cambridge one summer. He was an instructor on the Cambridge Radio Course, which I was taking as part of a two-year master's degree in theology and communication. By the end of the summer we had decided that we wanted to be 'friends', but, as planned, I went back to America and started the residential part of my study. I wasn't sure that I would ever see Chris again, and at that time I was extremely focused on my academic and professional pursuits. However, less than seven months later we were married, having only been on the same continent with each other for about three weeks in all! More of that story later, and back to the somewhat difficult beginning in our first proper home.

Even though I was very happy to be married to Chris, and I took to life in England very quickly, there was a rather painful time of adjustment. I was no longer surrounded by familiar people, places and things. Of course I wrote letters, and friends and family wrote to me, but it was different. There was also the telephone, but I did not want to use my precious time talking about how lonely I sometimes felt, or trying to explain that, even though I was happy, getting used to so many new things all at once was quite a challenge.

Also, I was proud. After all, no one had *ordered* me to marry Chris and move to England! I had freely made this decision, although it had not been easy. I had been aware of what the implications might be, and I didn't choose lightly to be separated from my former way of life. So I swallowed hard and watched myself learn to negotiate life in a new way as all my old crutches fell away.

One of the first differences I registered was that when I met new people they invariably asked me what my husband did. I was more than happy to tell them all about Chris, about how he was a radio producer, a trainer and a bit of a genius on the quiet in the way he crafted and wove together the various elements that go into making radio features. But after I had told them about Chris, their questions stopped. It didn't seem to occur to them to ask me about myself. Back in the States, this would have not only been odd, it would have been downright rude!

I was treated as if I had somehow been assumed into Chris's identity. By getting married, Chris had expanded his persona. By getting married, I had vanished. This was not a pleasant sensation, and I struggled to keep hold of my feelings of self-worth, as all the images of myself that I had taken for granted seemed to dissolve. It felt as if most of the person I had thought myself to be was disintegrating. I had to stop relying on people knowing my family, my Hamptons home, the boat, the schools and colleges I had attended, and even, because of my pregnancy, the way I used to look and dress. It was a moderately cataclysmic time of adjustment.

But I learned a lot. I learned how much of the way I had related had been dependent on shared experiences and a common knowledge of people and places. I realised how I had always assumed that people would be impressed with me because of some of my past achievements. However, the shorthand that had conveyed the correct messages in America could not be translated, and I was left without an effective way of establishing and communicating who I thought I was. All the little signals and triggers that used to work so effortlessly were now entirely ignored. It felt not only as if I had suddenly lost much of my value, but as if my ways of communicating had also been declared worthless. Things about myself that used to 'buy' me instant high status and recognition now went unnoticed.

I was thrown back onto a 'me' that I had never had to get to know before, a self without the fancy frills and accessories. I began to search for an understanding of myself that was based solely on my relationship with God. Of course, I had thought that my opinion of myself *was* based on what I believed, but it became clear that that was not the case. I soon realised that I was faced with a choice: either cling in desperation to an old way of judging my worth (and that clearly was not working), or let go of all my props and allow myself to discover who I was in a new way. I chose to release the old me.

As I loosened my grip on what I had held dear, I became increasingly vulnerable and tentative. All of a sudden, I wasn't so sure about *anything* any more. I began to ask God, 'Do *you* still love me? Am I still of value to *you*?' Not surprisingly, as my stomach grew larger, people did start noticing me, but the interest was now in me as a mother-to-be. Everyone wanted to know when my baby would be born and were happy to chat about the various details of pregnancy and birth. New friendships began to blossom, and I was grateful to have a common bond with so many other women.

Inside my mind, the questioning continued. 'Who am I?' 'Where is my life going?' 'How can I feel positive about myself again in my new relationships and roles?' As a Christian, though, I didn't want to start looking at who I was from a human point of view. Judging from the discrepancy between how I had thought about myself in the past and how I now viewed myself, I realised that my views were far too subjective. If my feelings of self-worth could be thrown so easily by getting married and moving to another country, then perhaps what I had been basing my self-worth on was more like sand than rock. I had to admit that I had allowed myself to be lulled into accepting a human evaluation of my worth, and when that changed, my sense of worth changed too.

I decided to start with God, and look hard at what our Creator had to say about humankind. I reasoned that if we ignored the divine perspective, then we would be missing out on the deepest possible understanding of who we are. I wanted to find out what it meant to say we have been made in the image of God. I wanted to see the relationships in my life in the light of my relationship with God. I wanted, in short, God's opinion, and not my own, because my own had let me down so badly.

I knew the Bible talked about putting off the 'old nature' and putting on the 'new nature', and I felt I needed to understand this for my new life. It had all made sense in America, but now it felt at times as if I had lost my faith as well as my identity. I knew I hadn't, but nothing seemed the same. I could not feel God's love for me the way I had before, and if I couldn't feel it, was it real? Was God still there to depend on? If I had ceased to have value in the eyes of those around me, did I still have value to God?

## Made in God's image

My explorations of what it means to be human and my attempts to answer the question 'Who am I?' are still continuing, but I have made some exciting discoveries along the way. I will start with the story of God making human beings on the sixth day:

> God said, 'Let us make man in our image, after our like-
> ness; and let them have dominion over the fish of the sea,
> and over the birds of the air, and over the cattle, and over
> all the earth and over every creeping thing that creeps
> upon the earth.' So God created man in his own image,
> in the image of God created he him; male and female
> created he them.' (Genesis 1:27)

There are a few things to notice. From the very beginning human-ity as a whole was seen to be made in God's image. There is some-thing about us, men and women together, that bears a resemblance to God. I doubt it is in how we look, since God does not exist in space and time, and therefore cannot have a body, or bodies, like ours. So in what way are we like God? At the risk of sounding simplistic, I believe we are like God primarily in that we have the capacity for love. As I described earlier, the internal dynamic in the Trinity is that of an endless giving and taking of love, and we, too, can give and take love.

The theologian Jane Williams thinks that being made in God's image is very much tied up with who Jesus was. She asserts:

> Jesus is what we were made to be, and in recognising Jesus as God's image, we are, at the same time, recognising our true selves. This spark of recognition, this extraordinary knowledge that we are made to be like God, is God's great gift to us, offered again and again in creation and recreation, and it would be false modesty to reject it and put all the emphasis instead upon our difference from God, how unlike God we are.[1]

If we have been made in God's image, we have also been created as part of the rest of God's handiwork. We do not live as aliens on our planet but as a part of the creation, as much as the birds and the bees. We exist in bodily form. I don't say that we exist *inside* our bodies, because our bodies are also part of who we are – whether or not we are happy with that thought! Who we are is a combination of body, mind and spirit, and to that we might also want to add heart and soul. The late writer and pastor Henri Nouwen believed that 'what makes us human is not our minds but our hearts, not our ability to think but our ability to love . . . We must give the heart pride of place as we try to discover and define who we are.'[2]

In the Psalms, King David expresses his sense of wonder at the mystery of his existence. He praises God for making him, saying,

> You created every part of me;
> You put me together in my mother's womb.
> I praise you because you are to be feared;
> All you do is strange and wonderful.
> I know it with all my heart.
> When my bones were being formed,
> Carefully put together in my mother's womb,
> When I was growing there in secret,
> You knew that I was there –
> You saw me before I was born.
> (Psalm 139:13–16)

Elsewhere in the Psalms, David observes that humans were made to be just a little lower than God and the angels!

Jesus also had quite a bit to say about our identity. If he were here to answer my questions, I believe he would stress, first and foremost, that our identity lies in the fact that we are loved. Because that sounds like such a passive stance, it is so difficult for many of us to believe that is enough, and to bother to discover what it really means.

It seems we have to work very hard for our hearts to believe and respond, and to value God's opinion of us. Even Desmond Tutu, the former Archbishop of Capetown, had to struggle with getting his heart to accept that he was loved, for himself, and not because he was a famous Christian leader. He described how he worked at reminding himself that he is loved, valued and of worth to God, no matter what role he might have.

> Usually I get up at 4 a.m. It's quiet and peaceful at that time, which I need to collect myself. It's a time when I try to engage with God. It's meditation. I try to centre myself on God so that he influences the rest of the day . . .
>
> During part of this time I kneel and then I crouch almost like a foetus. There is something about becoming a baby in the presence of God, being embraced, being dandled and being made to know that you are special and precious and loved.
>
> It's not because I can rush into Lesotho and out again, and appear on television; it's not because I'm an archbishop that gives me worth: worth comes as a gift from God, free of charge. I have gradually come to accept this. But constantly I have to be reminded, because I love to be loved so much.[3]

Our sense of self-worth is to be based on the understanding that God considers that we are worthy. God's love for us and the value he puts on who we are should be the basis on which we value ourselves. I'll probably say this several times, but it's worth remembering that nothing we can do can make God love us more, and nothing we can do can make God love us less. God's love for us is the rock we can place our trust in and from which we can take our sense of self-worth. It is the only thing that will never change. People, places, health, fitness and abilities all change, but God's love for us, his declaration that we are worthy, will never change. Even when all else is stripped away from us, that will never change, and God will never withdraw from us. It certainly might *feel* like it at times, but there comes a time when we have to decide. Will we trust our feelings, or will we trust what we believe to be true? When things are going well, our feelings augment our faith, but when things start to go wrong, our feelings tell us lies. That's why it's important to know what we believe, because we just may need to cling to it when the winds of change start to blow.

There are so many reminders in the Bible about God's love, and so many insights about our identities as those whom God loves. Over the years, I have gone through the Bible and made a list of all the things that are part of our God-given identities. The list is not exhaustive, but I think I have managed to find one or two clues. According to the Bible, we are:

- made in the image of God (Genesis 1:27);
- crowned with glory and honour (Psalm 8:5);
- children of God through faith in Jesus Christ (Galatians 3:26);
- brothers and sisters in Christ (Matthew 23:9; Hebrews 2:11; and elsewhere);
- corporately the Body of Christ (1 Corinthians 12);
- individual members of the Body of Christ (Romans 12);
- together we are one in Christ (Galatians 3:28);
- temples of the Holy Spirit (1 Corinthians 3:16);
- able, through the Spirit, to have the mind of Christ (1 Corinthians 2:16);
- given grace (Ephesians 4:7);
- given gifts (Romans 12:6–8;1 Corinthians 12; Ephesians 4:11);
- a new creation (2 Corinthians 5:17);
- free (2 Corinthians 3:17);
- discharged from the law (Romans 7:6);
- being changed into the likeness of Christ (2 Corinthians 3:18);
- not condemned (Romans 8:1);
- inseparable from the love of Christ (Romans 8:35 to end);
- the salt of the earth (Matthew 5:13);
- the light of the world (Matthew 5:14);

- adopted as God's children (John 1:12; 1 Corinthians 6:20; Romans 8:15);
- given a spirit of power and love and self-control (2 Timothy 1:7);
- heirs of God and fellow heirs with Christ (Romans 8:17; Galatians 3:29; 1 Peter 3:7);
- healed (Isaiah 53:5; 1 Peter 2:24; Psalm 103:3; Psalm 147:3);
- saved (Mark 16:16; Romans 8:24; Ephesians 2:5);
- known (Psalm 139; Romans 8:27).

Above all, we are loved, and there are so many verses that state this glorious fact that I can't possibly include them all! One of the best known is about God loving us so much that he sent Jesus, so that we might be able to live for ever (John 3:16). However, throughout both the Old and New Testaments, the theme of God's love for us runs like an unbroken golden thread.

There is much more I could find about who we are, but that's where I've got to so far. Remember, this list is true for all those who follow Christ, and many of the points are true for all people, whether or not they are Christians. Just by existing, we already have an amazing identity! I believe that we are so beautiful to God, and so much loved, that if we could see the whole picture of who we are, we would explode with joy.

We have all been given so much, and the tragedy is that, because of human sin and sometimes just because of accidents of nature, some people die without ever knowing how wonderful and amazing they are. Mother Teresa gave the poor and dying she ministered to a sense of how much God loved them. She was pretty clear about the identities of those she reached out to, and when they looked in her eyes they could see the love of Christ.

One of the things that we may well find ourselves doing in response to God's love for us is showing others the love we have been shown. I think there is something about God's love that prevents our acceptance of it from being entirely passive. The nature of love is that, once experienced, the impulse is to immediately begin to give it away! Love is not something we hoard in our lives and use when we need it, just to make ourselves a little more loving when it suits us. On the contrary, love tends to flood into our hearts and spill out onto anyone we happen to be near. This is why I do not think we can ever get too much love. The more we are given, the more we will want to give it away, and the more will come in to fill up what we have just passed on. Love is not a commodity, not something we have to keep in the bank and only draw out in reasonable amounts. Love, by its nature, tends towards excess. Perhaps we need to take more pleasure from the fact that we can eat too much, drink too much, get too much sun and work too hard, but we can never overdo love. Love is self-regulating, and its level is always full to overflowing!

I have tried to look at what I believe is true for human beings, created in the image of a loving God. I have tried to sketch a picture of what our identity as children of God might be. This, I hope, will help us to discover our God-given identities. In addition to this, there is also the question of the ways we are called to show God's love in our individual lives. Mother Teresa ministered to the dying in Calcutta. Jackie Pullinger brings the liberating love of Christ to the Triad members in Hong Kong. C. S. Lewis wrote books and gave lectures. John Tavener writes music that opens a curtain into heaven. Bruce Harris and others work to stop the murder of street children in Brazil. All these people, and so many more that we will never hear about, have discovered the main thing that they are meant to do with their lives. This is part of being called, something I go into later on, but it is also part of understanding who we are. How can we hear and respond to a call if we don't know who we are or what are our special gifts and skills, and how God wants us to use them?

I'm glad that most of us have lots of options in life. I think it's good that we aren't expected to do the same things that our parents or grandparents did before us. The downside of having choice, however, is that we have to decide. I think one of the most confusing things about life today is that we are told lies about how much we can do. One of the messages being communicated by our culture is that we can do everything we want to – and probably all at the same time!

You may have never thought that, but there was a time when I did, and it caused me a lot of anxiety. Part of why I fell for that message was because I didn't really know who I was or what I considered to be most important, and I ended up trying to do everything. I had to go through an exhausting, soul-searching exercise before I felt confident enough to make the right decision about my future. I have to say that I don't think we necessarily waste our lives if we head in a wrong direction, but I do think we will know much more peace and fulfilment if we bother to find out, as soon as we can, what it is that is most important to us. I also think that we might be of more use to God (although he does not judge us on whether we are useful!) if we are able to recognise what it is that makes us tick.

Things came to a head for me when I was faced with some tough decisions, and I wanted to discover two things: what was it that I cared most about, and how might God want to use my gifts and talents? In short, what were my special gifts and desires, and where was God leading me?

I had been teaching dance and choreographing in a private girls' boarding school called Chatham Hall. Chatham Hall is situated in nearly 400 acres of rolling Virginia countryside, and exactly how I had got there was quite a story in itself. But, there I was, a scant year after finishing my undergraduate degree.

My job was as the school's dancing instructor, and I was specifically taken on to choreograph the school's production of the musical *Godspell*. In addition, I had to chaperone the girls at dances and preach in the school chapel. The headmaster had also asked me to act as a floating, informal counsellor. Just be aware, I was told, and be there for the girls.

As the academic year drew to a close, I knew I had to make a decision. I had several options, all of which appealed to me greatly. First of all, I had been asked to stay on at Chatham Hall. Second, I had the choice of going to a law school in Washington DC. This particular law school appealed to me because it specialised in teaching jurisprudence. Jurisprudence is the study of law with an emphasis on what is just, or right, in any situation, not only what can or cannot be proved. I pictured myself becoming a latter-day King Solomon, the wisest of the wise, able to discern the right thing to do in every case, no matter how subtle or complex.

My third option was to stay in Virginia, and to spend more of my time on my voice. I had taken voice lessons for seven years, and had most recently been working with a wonderful teacher who wanted me to spend another year with her, before going off to Vienna.

There, I was to train for a further two years, before launching myself on the international opera scene.

I thought long and hard about these three options. Each had good points to commend it, and each also had its drawbacks. Staying at the school for another year was a delightful proposition. I loved the girls and my work, I got on well with the other members of staff, and it was a beautiful place to live. The downside was that I could not see myself meeting people other than those connected to the school. In particular, all the men were married, and the young men who weren't married were in school and a tad on the young side. I also really didn't like the thought of becoming so comfortable at Chatham Hall that I would be there years from then, Miss Muller the dancing instructor. It didn't quite sound like me.

Ms Muller the lawyer didn't sound much better either. Upon close reflection, five more years of hard slog lugging heavy books did not appeal. Being in the country's capital did appeal, but I felt that the process of becoming a lawyer, attractive as that was, would possibly kill off or subdue parts of me that I really didn't want to kill off or subdue.

So how about Miss Muller the opera singer? That would certainly be a creative choice, that would allow the expressive side of me to blossom. I loved to sing and act, and I enjoyed being able to move people to tears and laughter. But I was worried about whether I might become too self-absorbed. I could shut my eyes and see the bouquets of flowers thrown onto the stage after my performances, with rapturous cries of 'encore' rising above the tumultuous applause. I could also see myself complaining in rooms with draughts, banning smokers from my presence, and living out of suitcases for months of every year. It just seemed too selfish, too narrow and too unsettling a pattern for my life.

So what was I to do? At this time of having to make up my mind, my friend Heather Conley had to go to Chicago to do some postgraduate research, and she invited me to travel with her and to explore whether there were any courses I might like to take. We travelled by train from Washington to Chicago, a trip that took a couple of days, and as we travelled we spoke about our futures.

After hours of discussion, I realised that, above everything else, I wanted to communicate about God, and I wanted to do so freely, as myself, not playing a role. I wanted to be able to speak openly about God, as part of my primary work, not as a stolen opportunity outside office hours. I wanted to fight injustice, and be able to discuss issues of faith with people, and somehow I wanted to do all of this tied in with broadcasting and the media.

It was a breakthrough! At last I could articulate to myself what it was that I wanted to do! At last I knew what I cared most about!

When we got to Chicago, and then on to Wheaton, where Heather had to do her research, I was prepared to speak to someone from the postgraduate school, to see what courses they could offer. As it was, there was one that was exactly what I had been looking for. It was a master's degree in theology and communications. I had a quickly scheduled interview with one of the professors, filled out the application form on the spot, and on the following day was told that I had been accepted. I was also given another choice.

The two-year course began in September, and I was asked whether I would like to sign up for the summer school, to be held in London and starting in July. I could not think of any good reason why I should not begin as soon as possible, and so, there and then, I also committed to the summer course.

When I returned to Chatham Hall, I explained why I would not be staying, and they accepted my decision graciously. Two months later I flew to London, expecting a few weeks of intense study. I could not have known that within two weeks I would have met Chris, and that I would end up staying in England during August as well, to take the Cambridge Radio Course. I also could not have known that Chris and I would be married within seven months, and that shortly after that I would move to England and very soon be expecting our first child.

As I think back on the process that led to my decision to start further study, I realise that if I had not longed to discover what I really wanted to do, I could so easily have chosen any of the other options. If I had not ached to discern what God might want for me, I could have decided in another direction. I am sure God would have been able to use me no matter what I had chosen, but what happened to me at that multiple fork in the road was that I was eventually shown which way was the best way forward. It was worth all the effort, because I felt as if at last I was beginning to understand who I was and what God might have in mind for me.

I believe there are things we can do to help us to hear God's whisper and discern his call. Part of that is taking care of our bodies, and taking responsibility for our actions. I'm sure God never stops reaching out to us, but I think we can get ourselves into states where it is much more difficult ever to hear God.

We can remember to build time into our lives for simply *being* instead of *doing*, and in the being discover more of who God is and who we are. We can remind ourselves, when necessary, of the old cliché that life is not a dress rehearsal. Hopefully, this will inspire us to appreciate all of life, the mundane as well as the magnificent. We can develop the habit of prayer, listening to God as well as talking to God. We can be silent and allow God to tell us who we are and what he wants us to become.

I believe we have much more power than we generally acknowledge, power that can make things happen in our lives. Part of discovering God and ourselves is discovering this God-given power to make changes for good in our own lives and in the world around us. We can choose, after the initial shock, how we will respond to tragedy and failure. I have one friend who has been battling with cancer, and she tells me that she is actually thankful for what having cancer has taught her. She says she has grown much closer to God. I have another friend who has had the debilitating condition of ME for nearly ten years. She looks forward to being well and having her energy back one day, but she acknowledges that, if it had not been for the ME, she would never have taken the time to sort out some important issues in her life. Both these women responded to traumatic situations by slowly turning them upside down and inside out and coming out feeling grateful to God for what they had been able to learn through their illnesses.

In one sense we will never fully know who we are because we keep learning and growing all our lives. Every new person we meet, every new challenge, can reveal to us more of who we are and more of who God is. But we have to attend to our pilgrimages, and not expect someone else to make our discoveries for us.

Instead of ruminating over things we wished we had done differently, we can try to learn from our mistakes, ask for forgiveness for our sins, and start fresh at any time. Just as we know that energy cannot be destroyed, only changed, so we must learn that love cannot be destroyed. It may change shape or seem to disappear, but it cannot be destroyed. Sometimes, we will have to love in silence, because the person we care about cannot accept our love. Sometimes, we have to watch while someone we love chooses to walk a different path. But still we love.

I like to think that everything that we do in love is seen and known by the God of love. Even if we don't know what has become of our action, God does, and God remembers. God remembers, and knows the deepest desires of our hearts. Even before we can speak what is in our hearts and minds, God has heard and is longing to lead us onward. The adventure for us is to keep seeking God and to keep hunting for that which makes our hearts burn within. In doing so we will have discovered ourselves and come close to the Love that makes us who we are.

## 4

# How Then Shall We Live?

How then shall we live? That is the question. In the light of what I believe about God, about myself and about life, how should I live? The beautiful thought of continually responding to a loving God remains just that, a beautiful thought, unless it is somehow brought down to earth and translated into reality.

I will never forget the time I opened myself to God's love and nearly got drowned! I was seventeen and I'd been trying hard to follow Christ and be a good disciple, but I was failing miserably. It didn't help that there had been a lot of pressures in my life at the time – exams, money problems, family problems, boyfriend problems, you name it, it had all been happening, all at once!

I was visiting my aunt and uncle, Jan and John Payne, in San Dimas, California while looking around at universities. That evening friends gathered in their home for an informal prayer meeting, as they had been doing every two weeks for many years. It was lively and joyful and felt entirely natural. Towards the end of the evening there was a time for praying for each other. All of a sudden, Aunt Jan asked if I would like to be prayed for. I had been thinking a lot about my life, and I certainly wasn't happy with the way it was going.

As some of the people came over to me and put their hands on me and prayed, I began to feel the most extraordinary sense of God's love. I just sat there and let love deluge me in wave after wave. Not only was it pouring down, but it was filling me and surrounding me and permeating every cell of my body. I wept with joy and relief, and felt as if I was getting rid of aeons of pent-up hurt and worry and guilt. When it was over, I felt totally at peace, calm and completely loved. I knew without a doubt that God loved me. I knew, because I had experienced it, and my life was changed.

I do not believe it is possible to live a life that is pleasing to God or, ultimately, satisfying to ourselves, if we are not drawing on the love of God. If I may switch from a flood to a fountain, I believe we must drink deeply at the fountain of God's love. If we don't, we will shortly become thirsty and have nothing for ourselves or anyone else. My faith remains a fantasy if I do not make it real in my everyday life. My God has to be a God of Monday mornings as well as a God of weekends and holidays.

The only way I know how to live like this is to remain open to the Holy Spirit. The flood I experienced was the flood of the Spirit, and it altered how I saw myself and God. The Holy Spirit frightens some people, but I don't think we should be frightened, maybe awestruck, but never frightened, because what the Spirit brings in many forms is the fullness of God's love. The Spirit reminds us that God made us and set the planets spinning, and that maybe we don't know all there is to know about everything. It is also the Spirit who will lead us into all truth. The Spirit brings joy and delight, but also makes us wince with supernatural sensitivity when we have trod on someone's toes. Whatever we might like, we can never put or keep the Spirit in a box, because the Spirit is like water and wind and fire and will not be contained.

## Open to the Holy Spirit

Staying open to the Spirit may sound like a simple exercise, but in practice it requires courage and discipline; courage to be true to what we believe, and discipline in training our eyes and ears and hearts and minds to sense when the Spirit is moving. We need the Spirit's help in remaining open to God, and in being able to forgive and to receive forgiveness. We need the Spirit to protect us when doubt and failure pay us a visit.

With the Spirit's help I will see how clever I am at hiding behind masks and pretending to be something I am not. I will be able to look procrastination in the face and see it as the thief that it is. I will take responsibility for my health and lifestyle, while at the same time knowing full well that I exist in a state of grace. I will realise that all that I have and all that I am has been given to me by a self-sacrificing God who loved me to death – and beyond.

With the Spirit's help I will be able to assess my limitations with the eye of realism and love, and not give into the temptation to tell

God that my creation was a mistake. I will learn to love myself, and if I cannot manage that all at once, then I will live *as if* I loved myself. Even if I consider those around me to be a pain in various parts of my anatomy, I will treat them with the respect with which I wish to be treated. I will forego the temporary release of self-deception and the folly of blaming and shaming others.

I may fall down twenty times a day, but I will allow the Spirit to pick me up again. I will stop imagining that the world or any human being owes me anything, and I will open my hands and my heart to the healing sun – and flood of my heavenly Father.

Please do not think that I am entertaining the possibility that by doing all these things I might get life 'right'. Life isn't something that we get 'right' – or wrong, for that matter. We are either growing closer to God, or we are moving further away. Life is not only a biological reality; it is an unfolding, ongoing response to the One who is Love. I don't think we should even try to get life 'right', because if we do we will develop a rigid way of responding to people and circumstances, and the Spirit will feel trapped by our harsh manner. We will give ourselves, and everyone around us, an almighty headache that will affect all that life can be. With the Spirit's help we will aim for obedience, and settle for love. We may find as we go on that they are often one and the same. We will let the Spirit show us how to please God, and we will not make the mistake of presuming that we know best what will bring delight to God's soul.

## Defining love

Life will not be easy, but it is possible for it to be glorious and magnificent and extravagantly wonderful. Life is not neat and tidy, nor do we live it in black and white, but a million shades of grey and a billion shades of colour. The very fact of our existence, the world we live in, and the dimensions we can only dream about, are like cosmic explosions of colour and sound, tastes and smells – and touch. For if you count yourself a pilgrim on the path to life everlasting, you will need to be ready to be held and loved, stroked and calmed, squeezed and swung round by the God who is all love, all life and all beauty.

If life is not easy to pin down and turn into a formula it is because at the heart of who we are, who God is, and how we are meant to be living, is the risk and surprise of relationship. We were not created to live in solitude, untouched and unaffected by others, but to live in communion.

We can't do without relationships. The more babies are touched and held, the happier, calmer and more stable they are. Studies of World War II infant orphans showed psychological and physical stunting of those who had less human contact. Unfortunately, people who aren't touched much as babies don't touch much as adults, and the cycle of emotional neglect is passed on.[1] But touch is only good if it is loving. Being close to someone is safe only if they are able to give and receive love.

So, to tie down eternity to reality, we must always begin and end with love. Let's dissect love, and see what goes into it. In chapter 13 of 1 Corinthians, Paul gives a devastating description of love. Devastating, because it is so clear and straightforward that anyone remotely honest will realise how imperfectly they have loved. Paul states the ultimate impossibility of earthly possessions to make up for love. The God-given gifts of having all knowledge, a spiritual hot-line and faith itself are all worthless without love. Extravagant generosity is pointless if not done in love. Even death counts for nothing without love. Paul highlights and underlines, and even puts in bold, the point that if it is not done in love, it might as well not have been done.

Paul goes on to define love in sixteen different ways; eight in the positive, saying what love is, and eight in the negative, saying what love isn't.

| Love is | Love isn't |
|---|---|
| patient | jealous |
| kind | boastful |
| rejoicing in right | arrogant |
| long-suffering | rude |
| believing | insistent on its own way |
| hopeful | irritable |
| enduring | resentful |
| never-ending | rejoicing at wrong |

The list on the left reads like a dream wish-list – we can't match up – while the list on the right sounds all too familiar. Years ago a friend told me a simple exercise, to help me to see how I measured up to Paul's definition of love.

Replace the word 'love' with your name, or with 'I' so that the verses read, 'I am patient and kind; I am not jealous or boastful; I am not arrogant or rude, I don't insist on my own way; I am not irritable or resentful; I don't rejoice at wrong, but rejoice in the right. I bear all things, believe all things, hope all things, endure all things. My love never ends.' It's rather sobering.

Now try it again, this time using 'the Spirit', 'Jesus' or 'our Father' instead of 'love'. This way, we are reminded of the nature of God's love. It's impossible for us to live up to this description of love continually, but we can take heart that God is like this all the time and loves us this way.

## Developing discipline

The God I believe in has to be as real in the mundane, humdrum times as in the exciting and spiritually alive times. I have to relate to God on Monday mornings, as well as on the weekends or on holiday. Part of what helps me to live with a Monday-morning God is to develop some Monday-morning traits myself. I find I'm not naturally a very disciplined person. I get involved in many different things, and I like juggling and flitting from one thing to the other. For instance, sitting down and writing is often not easy for me. It would help if I could be chained to the chair, because I can find myself springing up for all sorts of obscure reasons, which become more obscure and more compelling on the days when the words are not flowing freely. Then, it is like torture as I make myself sit and write what I can. But I know if I didn't try, if I just said, 'Oh well, the muse isn't on me today,' I would write less and less, and I would not be opening myself to the inspiration that comes when I simply apply myself.

We cannot produce and create in our lives what we have the potential for doing if we try only when we are in the mood. We have to engage with the task even when there is no inspiration, for it is in the doing of our work that the inspiration often comes. Some people talk about a poem or a painting being 'given' to them, which can be an exciting and humbling experience, but most creative work is actually forged on the anvil of application. We need to allow the divine spark to ignite us and take us onto a new plane. I have to admit that most of my best results have come when I have given myself the time and space to think through carefully what it is I want to communicate, and when I have opened myself to hear the voice of the Spirit.

Perhaps you know the saying about success: 'Ten per cent inspiration and ninety per cent perspiration.' Yes, there needs to be a thought, an idea, or a picture in the mind, but the rest is down to the doing of it. In one of the many paradoxes of life, discipline helps to open us and keep us open to a process that is beyond our limited vision and purpose. If we believe that God is the source of all true creativity, then we can understand discipline as putting ourselves in a position to be open to the Creator.

It's strange, but discipline is one of those concepts that we all think we know about, but the way so many of us behave might indicate that we really don't believe that it is worth the bother. Musicians understand it, as do athletes, and almost anyone who has to perform in a way that is clearly beyond what anyone could do by just 'trying harder'. However hard we might try, unless we have put in the hours of practice over weeks and years, we will not be able to play the violin, run a marathon, do a backwards flip, walk on a high wire, perform a heart transplant, paint a masterpiece, or do any of the other feats of human endeavour which require extraordinary discipline, among other things. Discipline becomes a friend to those who submit to it.

I may know all this intellectually, but I still fight a running battle with my body and my will. Before I get up in the morning to go out for a run, I can almost convince myself that this morning is different; it wouldn't hurt if I just rolled over and went back to sleep. This morning, I need more time in bed, not out running. I fight this battle many mornings even though I know in my head that if I do not get up and go out I will not stay fit.

Happily, once I have been disciplined and got up, the results are usually impressive. Not only do I wake up quickly and feel better for being outside almost immediately, as I run I feel happier and more positive, sensations which can last for most of the day. For me, running is also symbolic for what I am trying to do in my spiritual life. I am trying to put God first, to give God time and to be in God's presence. This is where running and praying somehow begin to overlap. As I run I pray. Sometimes all I can do is ask God for strength, or admit to how I am really feeling about something, and most important of all, let God speak to me. Sometimes when I return, even if it's after just half an hour, I feel as if I have been away on a long journey.

One of the things that gave me the courage to keep on trying to form the habit of exercise was a stray comment made by someone who radiates health and who always looks in peak health and fitness. Knowing her to be a busy woman, I asked how she stayed in shape. She told me she got up at 5.30 every morning to do an hour of exercise. She must have read my mind, which was thinking, 'Ah, she's one of those people who likes that sort of thing,' because she then said to me, softly and simply, 'You know, I don't *spring* out of bed.' That's all she said, but it gave me the courage and strength I needed. If this queen of radiant fitness had to drag herself out of bed to exercise, then maybe there was hope for me. I simply had to start doing it, and carry on doing it, and the results would come.

It may be overly familiar, but I still warm to the truth in the saying, 'The journey of 1000 miles starts with the first step.' What I and many others seem to expect is that after the first step we will be 500 miles down the road! But that is not the case. We will be precisely one step down the road, but we will have begun. The task after that is to keep on going. Don't stop. Don't quit. Don't give up. Just keep going!

It was Calvin Coolidge, one of the former presidents of the United States, who said, 'Nothing in the world can take the place of persistence. Talent will not; nothing is more common than unsuccessful men with talent. Genius will not; unrewarded genius is almost a proverb. Education will not; the world is full of educated derelicts. Persistence and determination alone are omnipotent.' That quote inspires me, and I keep it stuck on the wall of my office, along with other sayings that both challenge and encourage me.

One of my favourites, also on my wall, is from Ralph Waldo Emerson, who said, 'Do the thing you fear and the death of fear is certain.' That simple sentence has spurred me on to pick up the telephone, put pen to paper and say things that otherwise I would not have said. It has inspired me to go way beyond my comfort zone and try hard for something that I wanted, but had been too frightened to attempt.

## Doubt

I would like to add a caution about spiritual discipline. Along with disciplining our bodies and our minds, it is obviously a good thing to bring some order to our spiritual lives. Many people make a practice of reading from the Bible every day, or reading Bible notes. Others have a time for prayer and for trying to hear what God's Spirit might be saying to them in the midst of a busy day. Some people go away on retreats at regular intervals, or attend various seminars and conferences. Certain practices and expectations grow up around the whole area of spiritual discipline, just as they do in the other areas of our lives. Some people think that to be truly spiritually disciplined, they must never entertain a moment of doubt. Doubt is seen as a sin. But I don't see it like that. Doubt is often the very thing that spurs us on to wrestle with what we really believe, and thereby refine our faith. Doubt may be unsettling and uncomfortable, like hunger, but just as hunger drives us to seek food, so doubt can drive us to seek the truth. If you find yourself plagued by doubts, try not to worry. Don't run away from them or deny them. Examine them, wrestle with them and ask God to help you to find a way through your doubting to faith. After all, God is bigger than our doubting, and is not thrown off course by our doubts.

Sometimes what we call doubt can be a way for God to speak new truth to us. We all get in ruts, and it can take a doubt to dislodge us from an old rigid way of thinking, and open us to a more responsive new way of seeing God. Once when Chris was making a radio programme he was knocked hard by some doubts. For about ten days he didn't know what to think about his faith. Then, slowly, he found his footing again, only this time the Rock he knew himself to be standing on was bigger and more solid than before.

Try to remember, you are in a relationship with the One who loves you more than you can imagine, the One who *is* Love. Surely, if you can trust God with your sin and sorrow, you can trust God with your doubts. Offer them to God as part of who you are, warts and all. It takes discipline to stay calm in the face of doubts, and to stay focused on your relationship with the living God, instead of on how you might be measuring up against a checklist of beliefs.

It might help to think of doubting more as serious questioning rather than lack of belief. It could be that your mind is not easily satisfied or reassured with something you cannot understand. Remember also what Matthew had to say: 'Ask, and it will be given to you; search, and you will find; knock, and the door will be opened to you. For everyone who asks receives, and everyone who searches finds, and for everyone who knocks the door will be opened' (Matthew 7:7-8).

I knew a man who boasted that he never had a doubt about his faith in his life. I also knew that his faith had stayed virtually the same for a number of years. Is that really what you want, to play it safe and never allow yourself to think the unthinkable? Of course, don't go chasing doubts, because they can be very undermining and tough to deal with, but don't be terrified of them. Constant doubting can cause you to lose your way, but never forget that God continues to hold you through thick and thin, through times of doubting as well as through times of great spiritual certainty.

There is a last caution about doubts: if we must not be frightened of them, neither should we be flattered by them. I know people who cling to their doubts and wear them like a badge of honour. The doubts have ceased to be real doubts at all, but idols, surrogate gods, fashioned from fragile egos and lack of courage. Real doubt always longs for a way through the darkness into the light of belief and trust. False doubts are used to keep God at arm's length, and to give out the message that the doubter is far more intelligent and sophisticated than others who believe.

False doubts do not seek God, only the justification of pride and disobedience. The person who says, with mock regret, that they couldn't possibly believe in the resurrection is a person who has never found that which was dead within them tremble and stir with the breath of new life. Such people have never really opened themselves to the healing, transforming love of Christ. Unfortunately, fear and pride, if given into over time, will damage the ability to discern the whisper of the Holy Spirit.

### Taking risks

If we are really alive, we will be taking risks. That means that at times we will fail. That's OK. Like our doubts, it might help to see failure in a different light. Remember that even Jesus appeared to fail along the way. Even he didn't manage to persuade everyone he met that he was the Son of God. The rich young ruler talked with him and listened to what he said, but he still turned and walked away. Now, we don't know what eventually became of him, but, on the surface, it looked very much as if Jesus had failed.

I think we need to see failure as part of what it means to be creative and human. The writer Murray Watts has had amazing successes and he has also known painful failure, yet Murray believes that the freedom to fail is also the freedom to live artistically. Among other things, Murray has written a number of scripts for film and television dramas. One script that he worked on for years was never used, because the film was never commissioned. Years of effort came to nothing.

Samuel Beckett once said that 'all art is failure'. The important thing is to try, to take the risk and *do it*. Whatever it is, throw yourself into it and do the best you can. It may succeed. It may not, but you will have known what it is to do something to the very best of your ability. Murray says that none of us can be a success all the time, but we can aim to fail in the most interesting way. *My, that's an exciting and fascinating failure!*

Peter was the apostle Jesus founded the Church on, the rock, and yet Peter is known for his dramatic failures. He was the one who denied Jesus, not once but three times. He was also the one who leapt out of the boat, and for a few steps found himself walking on the water towards his Lord. It was only when he looked down that he realised where he was, and he sank. But at least he stepped out. He had the impulse of faith, and while he kept looking at Jesus he kept walking.

In the story that Jesus told about the servants who were each given a certain amount of money to safeguard, the one who buried it was the one who came in for the master's criticism. The ones who risked investing it were praised, and yet they were the ones who had risked losing it.

I am painfully aware of many ways in which I fail. There are the letters I don't write, the calls I don't make and the routine chores I put off till 'tomorrow'. One of the threads that runs through much of my failures is the pernicious evil of procrastination. It is a sly beast and a dark magician, turning what seems like sweet reason into excuses and avoidance. I know only a few people who are not plagued with the scourge of procrastination to some degree, and these people are those who get the necessary and important things done – and then have time to do more! They are not always running to keep up. They are not always feeling stressed. I have to admit that they are also not the boring people I think I would like them to be, but just rather sane and more balanced than most.

Madeleine L'Engle tells the story of talking to a good friend about her feelings of failure with someone she loved. She bemoaned her failure and said that had she not failed, the person she loved would not have done something that proved to be destructive. Her friend listened to her tale of woe, and finally said calmly, 'Who are you to think you are better than our Lord? After all, he was singularly unsuccessful with a great many people.' Madeleine reflected: 'That comment, made to me many years ago, has stood me in good stead, time and again. I have to try, but I do not have to succeed. Following Christ has nothing to do with success as the world sees success. It has to do with love.'[2]

*I have to try, but I don't have to succeed*. Perhaps if we believed that we would not push ourselves too hard, and not be so cruel to ourselves. Perhaps we could give ourselves over to the task more freely and end up succeeding more often! What if we could be convinced that God is much more interested in the process than the outcome?

Sometimes I have tried to cheat a bit when I have to create something, whether it is an article, a sermon or a meal. I find I can often make something that is reasonably pleasing with not very much effort, but I know the difference when I have taken the time to work through a more costly process of creation. An ordained friend once said to me that he took a week to think about a sermon, an hour to write it and ten minutes to preach it. I wonder what his sermons would be like if he only bothered to think about it for ten minutes!

Whatever it is that inspires you to act, take the time and take the risk! It may be a raving success, or it may be an interesting failure. You will not know unless you try. Even if it isn't an earthly success, God will have seen what you put into it, and will know, whether in the process of your creating, you wove in love and joy.

I will never forget the last television interview with the poet John Betjeman. He was by then an old man and confined to a wheelchair, but he still had a sharp mind and a wicked sense of humour. The interviewer asked him whether he had any regrets about his life. Betjeman thought for a brief moment and then said with an impish grin, 'I wish I'd taken more risks – and had more sex!' Now that's the spirit!

## 5

## The Smile Within

When I was living with my family on the boat in the Bahamas we would frequently sail to remote islands that were nearly, but not quite, uninhabited. There were no proper jobs, and people had to eke out a living as best they could. Their main income was from fishing, but that required a seaworthy boat to be able to catch the fish and then transport them to a nearby island where they could be sold. The island inhabitants could also collect the beautiful pink queen conch shells, or the tiny shiny gold shells, and take them to be sold to tourists. Some of the women wove hats and baskets out of palm fronds, or hand-stitched little cloth dolls. They ate what they could grow in a soil that was very dry and sandy, and exposed to salt spray and harsh winds.

By our western standards they had little, but my overriding memories are of a people who would openly laugh as well as cry, who would welcome us with warm words and hugs, and who did not evaluate others by what they possessed. We were entering and passing through their world and they owed us nothing, and yet they went out of their way to care for us, the strangers in their midst.

Even though I was very young, I could tell when I was being treated as a fellow human being, and not as someone either to resent, envy or mock. I remember one of the things that seemed to amaze a lot of people we met was that it was just a married couple and their children aboard a small boat; no flash chrome gadgets and no other crew. My parents were genuinely open to people and responded in kind to the offer of friendship. There were so many hugs! There were hugs with people we had barely met, hugs with people who laughed in delight at the mere sight of our family, hugs with people who wept with joy when my parents would offer them one of the second-hand Bibles they brought with us to give out to people who had none.

If I squint my mind's eye and remember all those years of travel, two things stand out: the beauty and variety of the natural world, and the love and joy that we shared with so many people. It was as if wherever we went, Love had gone on ahead of us, there to greet us every time we pulled up at a dock or rowed ashore onto a beach. Oh yes, there were the oddballs and rogues, but there were mainly the outstretched hands and open arms, the wide smiles and gentle laughter.

I saw for myself that the love of God encircles the globe and fills all those whose hearts are willing. Yes, people from different cultures can be very, very different, but the lesson I learned was that kindness, generosity and compassion grow everywhere and are able to cross all aspects of human difference. That may sound idealistic, but I experienced it. The question is, how do we make that happen in our own lives at home, with the people we see time and time again, in the course of our everyday routines? How can we grow the fruit of God's Spirit wherever we are planted?

I believe the answer lies in cultivating a particularly large patch of joy in the soil of our freedom as children of God, warmed by the sun of Christ's love. The watering will be done more than adequately by the tears of our common suffering. We can learn to live through our heartbreaks and tragedies, confident that Jesus knows what we are going through; he has been there too. The difference for us is that his resurrection means that the darkness can never rob us completely of the light. We are the children of light, and if we follow Christ we will be walking in the light.

There will of course be times of sadness and great suffering, but having God's Spirit means that we can be kept from the finality of despair. No matter how dark our particular tunnels, if we lift our eyes and look, we can see the light. We can cling on to God's promise that he will never fail us or forsake us (Deuteronomy 31:6 and Hebrews 13:5). Remember also that Jesus did not come just so that we could endure a grindingly difficult or painful life. Jesus came so that we could live lives of abundance.

'Abundance' is a good word, because it means 'more than enough'. It implies provision beyond the bare necessities. We do not have to settle for a drab or bleak existence. Jesus came so that we might have lives filled to overflowing with goodness. This is the gift of God, offered to all. Whether or not we accept or reject the offer, the offer still stands.

Even the accepting or rejecting of God is not necessarily a once-and-for-all event. In small ways throughout our lives, in all that we do, we are continually saying either 'yes' or 'no' to God. There are some people who say a very big 'yes' at a specific point, and from then on know themselves to be pilgrims on the journey with and towards God. For many others, the response to God is an unfolding series of decisions and choices.

## Joy

So, how do we develop joy? How do we bring the abundance of the universe into our faltering, weary, complicated lives? How do we grow the smile within? I think some of the elements in the soil are a continuing wonder in the world around us, and an acceptance of who we are as beloved children of God. We need to recognise that we are unique, and learn what it is that brings us delight.

If we have a clear idea of who we are as beloved children of God, and if we are able to reach out in love to others, then that should make us extremely buoyant and joyful. We should be the ones who walk around spreading joy and goodwill wherever we go. We should be the ones who look as if we are having fun and celebrating just being alive. We should be the ones who everyone else wants to be friends with. Right? In the words of the Immortal Bard, *I don't think so.*

But if we really believe that God loves us, and if we have learned to accept that pain and suffering don't have the final word, then what is it that gets in the way of living as we believe we ought to live? Why isn't it possible always to pick the Christians out of a crowd of, let's say, tired commuters or harassed shoppers? Why doesn't our joy and peace hit others at twenty paces and leave them in stunned admiration and awe?

Part of the problem has to be that it takes a lot of effort for everyone, for Christians and non-Christians alike, just to cope with living in our modern world. In our so-called 'civilised' society, the hassle factor is all about filling in the right forms, paying bills on time, remembering to re-order the fuel, keeping MOT certificates up to date, not freaking when computers crash, and generally not forgetting a thousand and one little, but important, details that are supposed to help to make our lives run more smoothly. And that's the case only if we're lucky enough to have a job, a home, a car and a computer.

In many more places around the world, the day-to-day hassle revolves around getting enough water that's fit to drink, enough food and adequate clothing and shelter. Decisions about whether to re-decorate the kitchen, which model of car to buy or where to go on holiday don't really figure in most people's reality.

I have a sneaking regard for eccentrics, people who live their lives with a certain individual flair that sets them apart from the rest. I have known many and am related to more than a few. One of my mother's friends, Ruth, qualified for this distinct category. Ruth had been a society beauty in her youth and an accomplished writer, but when I knew her she dressed in faded second-hand clothes and lived in an old house filled with stacks of books and piles of papers. Ruth had had more than her fair share of problems, but she was constantly chuckling about something or other.

What I liked best about Ruth was an unusual decorating touch. All around her house she had placed small plastic dinosaurs: in the bathroom, in the pots of indoor plants and on the kitchen windowsill. Dinosaurs lurked everywhere for those with a sharp eye. The finishing touch was that Ruth had glued tiny lengths of bright green woollen yarn into some of the dinosaurs' mouths, so it looked as if they were munching grass. No matter how many times I saw them, Ruth's dinosaurs always made me smile. I'm not sure whether Ruth is to blame, but for many years now I have had a disturbingly similar habit of hiding little animals all around my house – minus the wool grass, I hasten to add.

One of the houses that Chris and I lived in was a small Tudor cottage that had been a schoolroom hundreds of years ago. The exposed indoor beams were riddled with large knotholes, about the size of mouse holes. Without knowingly having any overall design plan, I kept putting tiny felt or velvet animals into the holes, until the beams were teaming with little creatures. Like Ruth's dinosaurs, they made me happy. Every time I saw them, they gave me a quiet pulse of joy. Even when I was feeling dejected, something inside me still 'registered' the animals, and they managed to remind me to lighten up just a bit.

I have found that joy comes more easily when I surround myself with things that make me smile or that I consider beautiful. These days, in addition to placing small animals in holes in the walls, I have a fairly basic decorating rule: when in doubt stick it on the wall! It works for me. As a consequence, my walls sport a variety of objects: paintings, bits of antique textiles, a kimono, pieces of wood, old trays, fans, hats, even a section from an abandoned beehive. In a hallway there is a dead branch which always reminds me of the Wild West, especially the country around Santa Fe, where my brother Joel now lives. A bedroom wall is covered with two antique quilts that my mother gave me, one of them a family heirloom. On another wall I have hung a piece of broken trellis that looks like a cross.

Most of these things are just old bits and pieces that I have collected, or made or been given, but they all mean something to me. Recently, I was presented with a special 'thank you' gift from my church: a sculpture of Christ made out of a single branch. The slender figure, only about half a metre high, at times seems to me to be Christ rising from the tomb, and at other times I see him still hanging on the cross. It is so simple, in the way that many profound things are simple, and yet such an exquisite work of art that speaks volumes to me.

Something else that brings me joy is my collection of shells. Amazingly, my parents let me and Robin and Joel keep our best shells. When we came to leave our sailing life, they paid to have boxes of them shipped from the Bahamas back to our home on Long Island. Now, after years of living in cardboard boxes, my shells have their own shelves, and I get to see them every day. Looking at them always reminds me of how I found them, of my family and of days gone by. They also remind me of the beauty in nature, and of the miracle of this planet. They help to put perspective in my life. No matter what else is going on, my shells say to me, life is bigger and more amazing than you think; don't get so wrapped up in the crisis of the moment that you forget what life is really all about. My shells are a mark of God's presence in this world and his love for all he has made.

## Keep laughing

Some of the things I keep around me make me laugh and remind me of how we are called to come to God with the simplicity of little children. There is something healing and healthy about still being able to laugh and play, in spite of adult pressures and responsibilities. Once when I was out walking I found an old piece of moss-covered fence by the side of the road. I lugged it home and hung it on the wall, and placed an inscription beneath it that read 'I took a fence.' Friends would sometimes ask me what it was, why I had a bit of old fence stuck to my wall. I would point to the title I had given it, and most, not all, would get the play on words. Eventually the moss dried up and stopped being green and the wood disintegrated, and I had to dismantle this fine work of art, but while it was with me it gave me immense pleasure. Even thinking about it now brings a smile to my face.

In fact this silly fence has had a lasting effect on me. In the middle of the night not so long ago, I couldn't get to sleep and found myself thinking about 'I took a fence' (say it out loud!). I started to laugh and soon began to laugh so hard that I woke up Chris, who had been sound asleep. He immediately thought I was sobbing, and asked me worriedly what was the matter. I had to confess that I was thinking about my wonderful *objet d'art*. I apologised for waking him up, but explained that I just couldn't help it. By then I was weeping with laughter. Chris started laughing too, and we lay there in bed in the middle of the night laughing and laughing, with tears running down our faces, all because of a piece of old fence I had once hung on the wall.

Some may think this is slightly mad or sad, or possibly both, but I think this is healthy and sane, a clear reaction of joy pushing through the tangled underbrush of my heart and mind and surfacing with gleeful abandon. Bad timing, maybe, but good for the soul! I think that each of us needs to discover the things that make us happy, and then bring them into our lives. Whether it's bits from nature, certain pieces of music, types of food, even specific colours, we can incorporate them into our lives to remind us of the joy God feels in creation. It needn't be an expensive proposition, but it has to work for each individual. Happily, many of the things that bring me this type of joy are free. So much the better!

I believe that these moments of joy are all around us, waiting to be let in to our consciousness. When we welcome them they can lift us, even briefly, so that we see that life is not all doom and gloom, that there is always something to be thankful for, something to look forward to and something to wonder at, or even something that can make us smile.

My friend Kate has been bowled a fair number of googlies in her time, yet she responds to life with almost heroic optimism. Above all, she has an immense capacity for getting excited by new ideas and possibilities, as well as the courage to take risks. For a while we met almost daily over several months to work on a business project that Kate had initiated. It happened to be when *Dad's Army* was being shown on television. One of the characters in the series was a Scottish man who, in response to just about everything, would cry out, 'We're doomed!' Kate's little son Benjamin had seen the programme and had picked up the catchphrase. He would run around the house, shouting at the top of his lungs, in a heavy Scottish accent, 'We're doomed, we're doomed!' He had, of course, no idea what it meant.

When he did it during the times Kate and I were working together, we could not carry on. We would stop our earnest deliberations and laugh till we cried. The spectacle of an energetic and carefree little boy yelling out a message of doom cut instantly across whatever problem we were discussing, and in those days there were many problems to discuss. To this day, whenever we stub our metaphorical toes, we still occasionally bellow 'We're doomed!' It has the immediate effect of making us feel much *less* doomed. I invite you to try this, and I can guarantee it works, but only if you shout loudly and use a Scottish accent!

## Holiness

I believe having the type of joy inside that bubbles up unexpectedly is somehow tied in with being holy. Don't let that scare you! I promise I'm not suggesting an ascetic lifestyle or a lifelong regime of poverty, chastity and obedience (although, come to think of it, that has worked for thousands of people). Rather, I have come to understand holiness as a result of our spiritual positioning. Being, or becoming, holy isn't something that we have to strive for. It is not the province of naturally virtuous people. Holiness is what happens when we stay close to God. We become holy the more we allow the Spirit's loving power to heal us and make us whole.

It is not something that we can earn, or save up for, like supermarket saver points. Three years of clean living and, hey presto, an extra helping of holiness! I really don't think it works like that, even though you may have run into people who would have you believe that it does. Holiness does not happen just because we dot our 'i's and cross our 't's. In fact, that will probably work against it, because with holiness the focus is all on God. Not, how am *I* doing? Not, what are *they* up to? Holiness comes from an ability to let God love us.

Holiness is another one of those paradoxes: the more we let God love us, the more we can only see God, and the less likely we will be to even think about our own holiness. Holiness is God's gift to those who can recognise it and receive it, not to those who qualify for holiness in some way.

No one qualifies for it. All we can do is receive it. We do not have to wait until we are old and grey, or until we have been to the right churches or read the right books. It is part of the abundance of God, waiting to be poured into our lives until our hearts are overflowing.

That's why I reckon that joy has something to do with holiness, because being that open to God will mean that we will be more and more drawn into God's great Dance of Love, which, I imagine, is pretty joy-making.

Mother Julian wrote that our destiny is 'endless joy', and she went on and on about if only we knew how much God loved us, then we would never worry. In one of her visions of Jesus she saw that he looks at us with 'blessedness and joy' and also with 'compassion and pity'. But, she observed, 'the joy and blessedness surpassed the compassion and pity as heaven surpasses earth.'[1] We cannot even imagine how much God loves us or how wonderful it will be to live as one with him. It is beyond us, and yet we can trust in the reality of finding endless love when we live close to the heart of God.

### Keep looking

There is wonder and beauty to be seen, but we have to look. We have to be open to seeing beauty where we do not expect it. In being open to the extraordinary in the ordinary, I think that we are opening ourselves to God. God may have come to Moses in a highly visible burning bush, and God may still come to some of us in fairly obvious ways, but I believe most of us discover God in our lives when we get into the practice of looking for him in the things we usually take for granted.

If you have a set pattern of how you travel to work or college, start noticing things along the way. Look for signs of beauty and life. Perhaps you will spot a vase on someone's windowsill that will suddenly seem to be bursting with beauty. Perhaps you will see in the face of a passing child a glimmer of compassion or secret joy. Perhaps you will notice in a shop window the colour of something that makes you feel strangely alive. Try to get in the habit of opening up and responding to these signs of God's presence.

We won't know it, but I believe our holiness will draw other people, because it really isn't ours at all. Rather, people will somehow sense the inexplicable love of God, and they will want more of that love. This is the way we can all spread the good news of Jesus Christ. As St Francis supposedly said, 'Go and preach the gospel to all you meet. Use words if you must.'

Holiness is a sign of closeness to God, and that will communicate more quickly about God than thousands of worthy words or well-meaning pamphlets, although words and pamphlets have their place. Emmanuel Cardinal Suhard once said that to communicate about God 'does not consist in engaging in propaganda, nor even in stirring people up, but in being a living mystery. It means to live in such a way that one's life would not make sense if God did not exist.'[2] Would my life make sense if God did not exist?

How difficult, or rather, how costly. When things are going well, and others smile upon my efforts, then being a Christian seems eminently reasonable. But holding on to God, burrowing deeper into God's embrace when the world is saying I am misguided or foolish, that is not easy.

Another thing, I don't think that living a life responding to God's love is the sole province of the Christian. There are those of other faiths who are earnestly seeking wisdom and truth. Far too often we Christians get smug and try to dictate to God, and to each other, where and when and how God will work. We forget how big God is, how much he loves all that he made, and how he aches to be known by everyone, not just the likely candidates, that is, the ones of whom we approve. I don't mean to imply that it doesn't matter whether or not we respond to the call to repentance and the promise of new life. I believe it does matter: I believe that Jesus shows us, and *is,* the Way, the Truth and the Life, as well as our only hope of salvation, but this does not mean that God's Spirit cannot and does not blow where it wills. God is looking for open, humble receptive hearts. Everywhere, with everyone. Who is making space for God in their lives? Who is noticing the flickers of joy that come as God breathes life into our beings?

I think we need to rediscover the art of *being,* if we are ever to grow joy and become holy. How often do you give yourself permission to do those things which free your mind to think beyond your 'to do' list? Are you able to sit or wander around and *do* nothing without feeling an identity crisis coming on?

If this is an area where you struggle, take heart! You are not alone. I suspect there are many of us who are driven to activity and purpose in a way that has created an unbalanced life. I know in the last chapter I stressed the need for discipline, and I stand by what I said, but part of our discipline (another paradox) will be to learn when to sit lightly to all our activity and allow ourselves to *be.*

I was recently sent a poem by my friend Arthur Harcourt, composer, songwriter, poet and retired headmaster. Using only three different lines to create four stanzas, Arthur has written a simple and beautiful work of peace and meditation. When I read it I am helped to take delight in *being.*

Quiet

Now is my quiet come again
Deep in the music of my song
The stillness I had lost so long
Now is my quiet come again

Deep in the music of my song
The stillness I had lost so long
Now is my quiet come again
Deep in the music of my song

The stillness I had lost so long
Now is my quiet come again
Deep in the music of my song
The stillness I had lost so long

Now is my quiet come again
Deep in the music of my song
The stillness I had lost so long
Now is my quiet come again

## 6

## When It All Goes Wrong

If only life could always be filled with love, joy, peace and the ability to sit lightly to one's problems, but it's not like that. We get depressed, we get ill. People whom we love leave us or die. We experience rejection, violence, cruelty and neglect. We trip up, physically, mentally, morally, ethically and psychologically. For some, just being alive hurts, and the pain seems unrelenting.

Madeleine L'Engle has this to say:

> Being a Christian, being saved, does not mean that nothing bad is ever going to happen. Terrible things happen to Christians as well as to Hindus and Buddhists and hedonists and atheists. To human beings. When the phone rings at an unexpected hour my heart lurches. I love, therefore I am vulnerable.[1]

Being vulnerable, being able to be hurt or wounded, is part of being human.

### How we see ourselves

I saw a documentary on television about how disabled people in the UK were treated in the middle and earlier parts of the twentieth century. The disabled people, most at the time of the programme in their sixties and seventies, spoke with amazing candour about the appalling things done to them when they were children. A woman with dwarfism told how she had been hung on ropes in the mistaken belief that it might increase her height. A deaf man spoke of how he had been sent away to a special school when he was a child, and how desolate and abandoned he had felt. Person after person recounted their stories, some in a matter-of-fact way, some with sadness, but all without bitterness. What struck me more than anything was their dignity and strength. Many of them had been told that they would not live beyond childhood, and here they were, triumphantly elderly and still full of life. They were the exceptions. Stories were also told of how many disabled and disfigured people of that time did not survive their ordeals, victims less of their physical disabilities than of other people's mental and emotional cruelty.

What was it that was so special about the people who had taken part in that documentary? Certainly, they had been exceptionally brave, but perhaps it was that they seemed to have a greater degree of self-esteem and self-acceptance than many people without any disabilities.

I have met young women who are physically close to perfection, and yet who have trouble loving and accepting themselves. They battle with a poor self-image and low self-esteem. They turn against their bodies and starve them or stuff them in a desperate attempt to gain some degree of control over their lives. They punish themselves with obsessive exercise or other behaviour. They cut and harm themselves in the hopes that physical pain and blood-letting can help their inner agony to bleed away.

I know of young women, and men, who believe the lie that academic achievement indicates their worth, and sometimes the pressure drives them to take their own lives. I know of others who are destroyed by the taunts and bullying of their peers, and they decide life is not worth living.

I have successful, intelligent adult friends who still struggle with overwhelming feelings of unworthiness and failure. I meet people who have given up on themselves, and who have given up on life. Their very existence seems to mock them. They are in inner despair.

Often, the experience of suffering has little to do with what is on the outside, and everything to do with what is going on inside. If we could only change our thoughts, our opinions, we could see life, and ourselves, in a whole new way. That's what Jesus did for us. He showed us what God thought about life and about us. Each of us is worth dying for, each of us has infinite value.

Because of Jesus' life and death, and most particularly, his resurrection, there is the hope and the chance of new life, a new way of looking at ourselves, a new way of looking at other people, and a new way of relating to God. 'If anyone is in Christ, there is a new creation: everything old has passed away; see, everything has become new!' (2 Corinthians 5:17). We become new in this sense first by accepting what Jesus did, and then by asking the Holy Spirit to come into our lives. Not everyone gets flooded, as I was, but all who have welcomed the Spirit will discover a fountain within. Sometimes it may feel as if it has dried up, but it never does completely. A contrite heart, a cry for help, a response to love, and the water will bubble up again.

How we see the world and ourselves was initially shaped by what we learned when we were children. What messages did you learn as an infant and as a young child? Did you know deep down, not in an intellectual way of knowing, but in the very core of your being, that you were loved and accepted? Were you neglected, ignored, ridiculed? Were you helpless in the face of your parents' anger or violence? Were you treated like a thing instead of a person? If so, you will have to work hard at learning new messages about yourself.

Remember what your true identity is and make the choice to believe the best about yourself. No matter what you have done or experienced already, no matter what you may do or experience in the future, God loves you. Nothing you do can alter God's opinion of you. Nothing that has happened to you can affect how God sees you, except perhaps to increase his compassion and the depth and breadth of his mercy.

One of my friends, whom I shall call Ginny, took on the daunting task of working through the knowledge that she had been the victim of abuse when she was a little girl. Throughout her brave struggle to be freed from the pain and damage of the past, she clung on to the fact that she knew her mother had always loved her and she knew her friends loved her. Increasingly, she experienced God's love in ways that cut through and began to dissolve the fear she experienced in nightmares and towards men.

One night she had, not a nightmare, but a very realistic dream about being in a beautiful garden with Mary Magdalene. Mary Magdalene held her and hugged her, and Ginny felt more safe, secure and happy than she had ever felt before. When she awoke, the feelings of love and security from the dream were still with her, and she felt as if a genuine, healing encounter had taken place. The dream reoccurred several times, and gradually Ginny's memories and scars began to be healed. Intellectually, Ginny already knew that God loved and accepted her, but she needed to experience God's love for her as a little girl.

A further breakthrough came during another dream, when Jesus came into the garden and Ginny was able to let him hold her. Jesus had entered the dream before, but previously Ginny had not even been able to hold his hand. At last, the little Ginny was able to climb into his lap and let him hug her.

It took a long time, much perseverance, many friends and helpers, and many tears, but Ginny is now free from crippling memories of her past, terrifying nightmares, and free also from her fear of men. It wasn't just the dreams, but they were a significant part of Ginny's healing process, a process from which she could have pulled back at any time along the way. But she stuck with it with incredible courage, continually taking the risk of opening herself in new ways to the healing touch of God's love.

If we remain open to God and persist with even a shred of hope, God will come to us and let us know how much we are loved, even if it is in ways we would have never thought possible. But part of accepting God's love is letting go of the old ways of seeing ourselves – and that is scary. There are moments in our lives when we are like trapeze artists, and we have to let go of the swing we are holding in order to reach out for a new swing or the hands of another trapeze artist. If we cannot let go we will never move on, never change. It is like a small death; we have to say goodbye to the past before we have quite seen or been able to grasp the future. It is another leap of faith, another leap further into God.

Whatever it is that is holding you back from experiencing God's love, God knows about it and is waiting for you to open your heart and trust him enough to let him heal you. For Ginny, it was a long process, and while she will never be free from the reality of her past, her past no longer has any power over her. More than that, through the series of dreams, God was able to heal who she *was*, as well as who she is now. God, who exists outside of time as we know it, is able to enter our lives at any point and heal our present as well as our past.

## When we sin

But what if our problem is not so much being sinned against as in sinning? What if we know ourselves to be the cause or even part of the problem? After committing both murder and adultery, King David wrote a psalm confessing his guilt, begging for God's mercy and asking God to restore him:

> Remove my sin and I will be clean;
> Wash me, and I will be whiter than snow.
> Let me hear the sounds of joy and gladness;
> And though you have crushed me and broken me,
> I will be happy once again.
> Close your eyes to my sins and wipe out all my evil.
> Create a pure heart in me, O God,
> And put a new and loyal spirit in me.
> Do not banish me from your presence:
> Do not take your holy spirit away from me.
> (Psalm 51:7–11)

The first step is to acknowledge our wrongdoing to God, and the next step is to accept the forgiveness that God already extends to us. However, unlike King David, we can look at Jesus and know more deeply and fully that we have been forgiven. The fact that I may not understand exactly how that happened, or even why it was necessary, is not important. The full meaning of the cross remains a mystery so great and so profound that every time we think of it, we can see and understand new things. Jesus is our example, our guide, our goal and the Way we follow. As I said, it's a mystery.

For now, for the rest of our earthly lives, we will still commit sins, but our old nature is transformed. New possibilities for a new relationship with God open up. The amazing imagery of the curtain in the Temple in Jerusalem being torn from the top to the bottom at the moment when Jesus died, speaks of God ripping away in a divine act of righteous violence what had been separating him and humanity. It is gone, the barrier is no more. There is the possibility for a new openness, the chance to become one with God in a way that had not been possible before. Too many millions of people over the past two thousand years have experienced something of the effects of what happened on the cross for it to be an empty myth. The cross is not just a tragic mistake, frozen for ever in history, but the means for all people to become who they were meant to be.

Alas, the tendency to sin is an undeniable part of being human. But there are ways of looking at sin that I believe can help us to put it into God's perspective. Mother Julian looked at sin as the process of taking away some of the good of what we were created to be and producing instead something like a cosmic black hole. Seen that way, sin becomes a deficit, a negation of our true identity as beings made in God's image. The solution is not to concentrate on our sin as if it were some unwelcome aspect of who we are, but rather to see it as something that takes away from, that negates, our truest selves. Another way of looking at sin is to see it as an accretion to our deepest, beautiful inner selves. J. Philip Newell, a Scottish writer on contemporary spirituality, considers that 'the essence of who we are has not been erased by sin but covered over by sin'.[2]

Our sin, as real and despicable as it is, does not make God hate us, and so it should not make us hate ourselves, but should make us run even harder to God to ask for forgiveness and for help to be stronger, wiser and more obedient.

Mother Julian puts it beautifully:

> Though we sin continually he loves us endlessly, and so gently does he show us our sin that we repent of it quietly, turning our mind to the contemplation of his mercy, clinging to his love and goodness, knowing that he is our cure, understanding that we do nothing but sin.
>
> If there be anywhere on earth a lover of God who is always kept safe from falling, I know nothing of it – for it was not shown me. But this was shown: that in falling and rising again we are always held close in one love.[3]

We cannot talk about suffering and sin for too long before we are faced with the question of evil. The great King David was extremely concerned about it:

> Examine me, O God, and know my mind;
> Test me, and discover my thoughts.
> Find out if there is any evil in me

And guide me in the everlasting way.
(Psalm 139: 23–24)

But what is evil, and is there a devil? C. S. Lewis was often asked whether he believed in a devil, and this was his answer in the preface to *The Screwtape Letters*, his witty and insightful book composed as a series of letters from the devil to his nephew, a trainee demon on earth:

> The commonest question is whether I really believe in the Devil. Now if by 'the Devil' you mean a power opposite to God, and, like God, self-existent from all eternity, the answer is certainly No. There is no uncreated being except God. God has no opposite. No being can attain a 'perfect badness' opposite to the perfect goodness of God; for when you have taken away every kind of good thing (intelligence, will, memory, energy, and existence itself) there would be none of him left.[4]

Lewis did not believe in the Devil as an opposite power to God, but he did believe in evil.

The existence of evil, however one chooses to define it, is all too blindingly obvious. It is the inevitable consequence of the reality of free will. If we are to respond to God's love freely, then there must be the possibility of genuine choice. God did not create evil, or anything that is evil, but he did create the possibility that people are free not to choose him. Evil is the result of choosing to say 'no' to God, choosing not to belong to God.

The thought of a distinct being that is entirely evil, the devil, creates more problems. As Lewis said, whatever the devil is, the devil is not God's opposite number. With God, there is no opposite number. The devil might be described, then, as a malignant personal force that seeks to bring chaos where there is order and darkness where there is light. The devil exerts evil force, and is assisted by demonic spirits that wreak havoc in human lives.

Having said this, there are many who find it more helpful not to waste too much thought or energy on the concept of the devil. If there is a devil, they argue, then he, in common with all created things, was created by God, and ultimately he will have to answer to God. As Martin Luther said, 'The devil is God's devil.'

My psychotherapist friend Karina believes that 'all that the devil could throw at us, he threw at Jesus, and we know from the resurrection that God's love is stronger than anything of the devil, even death.' I happen to know that Karina has had more than her fair share of evil forces trying to undermine her, but she is adamant that they are not real in the way that God's love is real. Her life, like many people's, may have been buffeted by evil, but Karina sees it as her greatest challenge to keep herself open to God and to choose, moment by moment, to hang onto the positive, the way God sees us.

In eternal terms, evil is hollow and ultimately futile. Until God finally establishes his kingdom of love, we still have to exist with evil, but we can choose to turn our attention more and more to God, and rob evil of our attention and thought. We will still be hurt by evil, we still have to be on guard against it, but we can think of it in the context of the greater reality in which evil and the whole realm of darkness is vanquished. Like Karina, we all face the challenge of living in the belief that God's love has *already* won.

But how do we do it? In the middle of suffering and pain, how do we keep our eyes on God's love and ultimate victory? Can we ever be safe while we still exist as earth-bound humans? Do we really have any power over evil?

I believe the key to the answer of all these questions lies in the continuing activity of the Holy Spirit. We not only have the words and promises of Jesus, and the conviction that God's kingdom one day will come, but we also have the presence of the Holy Spirit. We have God in us, the fountain and the flood, the protecting Father, the compassionate Mother, the wind and fire which no evil can withstand.

We have been given the power and ability to discern whether or not someone is speaking by the power of the Holy Spirit. One of the tests is whether the person can confess that Jesus Christ came in the flesh (1 John 4:1–3). Knowing how to tell if a spirit is of God is good news in a society that, in general, casually flirts with the occult and does not take the power of evil seriously. Yet every day we read in our papers, hear on the radio and see on our television screens the outworking of evil in our world. We do not even have to resort to the media; we can talk to our friends and observe in our own lives the effects of humanity's brokenness, estrangement from God and wilful disobedience to the One who said 'Follow me'. Even worse, there are people who have chosen the darkness over the light, and they bend their energies to actions that are only leading them further and further from the lasting Truth.

The spirits of darkness are not part of Christ and cannot add to the light. If you have had anything to do with the occult, it is important to tell God what you have done, ask for God's forgiveness and protection and get rid of any occult objects or books that you may have. When I have discovered certain things with a spiritually unhealthy sense to them I have either burnt them or thrown them in the bin, and I also pray for God's protection.

A few years ago my daughter Angela and I travelled to America for the wedding of my oldest friend, and Angela's godmother, Marilyn Seabury Root. We had a day or two to spend after the wedding, and so we visited a small resort on the East Coast. Angela was very keen to buy presents for her friends, and we went into shop after shop along the high street. I began to notice that many of the shops were selling occult jewellery, odd little statues and other objects. I asked Angela to hurry up and finish her gift buying.

Angela was not impressed with my spiritual intuition, and she carried on. However, we entered one shop, and there sitting on the floor in front of us, just humming and rocking, was a disturbing looking man. He was young, but his face was extremely old and he stared up at us with strange eyes. This time Angela picked up the strong vibes, and we quickly got out of the shop.

Angela was very shaken, and she told me she had finished her shopping. Later that night, she came into my room, very frightened. She said she had not been able to sleep, and she asked me what was wrong with the man. I told her that I thought he was probably harbouring an evil spirit, and that many of the shops we had been in earlier that day had actually seemed to me to be buzzing with occult energy.

I spoke with her in greater depth than I ever had before about the spiritual realm, the Holy Spirit and about what Jesus had accomplished by his death. At the end of my explanation, Angela said, 'Now I understand why we need Jesus.' Indeed. But I was also able to let Angela know that we were completely protected. We prayed together and Angela spent the rest of the night in the spare bed in my room.

Until you meet evil like that, it is easy to scoff, but once met, never forgotten. It is not possible to describe what was different about that man: why, for instance, he could not have just been high on drugs, or suffering from a mental handicap. But there was a difference, and it is unmistakable. At times like that I am particularly grateful that God has conquered all evil. Even though its power is not real in the way that the everlasting power of God's love is real, nor is the power that evil can exert worthy of being compared with the power of the One who created and sustains all of life, it can still take hold of those who either welcome it or who do not know what they are doing. Thank God for Jesus and the Holy Spirit!

At other times when I have been frightened, I have found that saying the name of Jesus gives me peace and brings a sense of protection. We are told in the gospels that the disciples healed people and cast out demons in Jesus' name, and that his name, in itself, has power. It is a verbal defence against any force ranged against us, and we can be confident that it is by far the strongest. Sometimes, in addition to saying Jesus' name, I pray in unknown words, what St Paul calls 'tongues' in his letters in the New Testament. Tongues are one of the gifts of the Holy Spirit listed in 1 Corinthians 12:4–11, along with others including faith, wisdom, healing and prophecy. There has been much controversy about tongues, but I have found them to be a powerful weapon against extreme fear.

I also find that reading the Bible helps to calm me when I am frightened. Some of the psalms have beautiful promises: 'The Lord will keep you from all evil; he will keep your life. The Lord will keep your going out and your coming in from this time forth and for evermore' (Psalm 121:7–8). There is also Psalm 91, which is filled with rich images of God's faithfulness:

> You who live in the shelter of the Most High,
> who abide in the shadow of the Almighty,
> will say to the Lord, 'My refuge and my fortress;
> my God in whom I trust.' . . .
> You will not fear the terror of the night,
> or the arrow that flies by day,
> or the pestilence that stalks in darkness,

or the destruction that wastes at noonday.
A thousand may fall at your side,
ten thousand at your right hand,
but it will not come near you.
(Psalm 91:1–8)

I also remind myself of what Paul wrote to his young friend Timothy, 'For God did not give us the spirit of fear, but of power, love and self-control' (Timothy 1:7).

Hold on to Christ, hold on to life. Circumstances can and do change, and by the grace of God we can know peace. In any situation there is always hope. Call out to God and let the Holy Spirit work in quiet. Be patient; God is unfolding your future, but you must not run ahead and miss the better way. God will never give up on you. Never. It is not in his nature to do so. It is always worth persevering through the darkness, because we have been given the promise of dawn. Let every morning remind you that, as the sun rises without fail, even if at times it is hidden behind clouds, so God loves you without fail. God's love is the only power that will last, and we have that power in us if we open our selves and ask Christ to live in us.

For the times when we are frightened, for ourselves and for others, we need to remember that 'there is no fear in love, but perfect love casts out fear' (1 John 4:18). When we allow God to fill us with his love, there will be no room for any darkness or fear, and we will know the peace of God that passes all understanding.

## Being positive

There are other things that we can do to give our energies to all that is positive and to combat fear. One thing is to develop the practice of thinking and even speaking out loud positive thoughts, or repeating and memorising verses from the Bible. If we say them frequently enough, they sink into our subconscious, and go to work inside us, where other parts of our minds can't tell us we're wasting our time!

Counsellor and writer Louise Hay suggests saying positive thoughts, or affirmations, in the mirror. She reasons that as children we probably received most of our negative messages from people standing very close to us and looking us straight in the eye. She has discovered that many adults still give themselves negative messages when they look at themselves in the mirror. 'We either criticize our looks or berate ourselves for something. To look yourself straight in the eye and make a positive declaration about yourself is, in my opinion, the quickest way to get results with affirmations.'[5]

I've tried this, and at times I've unexpectedly ended up in tears. I think many people hide what's really going on inside by trying to deny or bury painful emotions. But, of course, hidden problems don't go away, they just eat away at us on the inside and occasionally resurface in all sorts of unacceptable ways. Often I find myself saying a certain Bible verse over and over again. Sometimes I don't even consciously choose which verse to say; it chooses me. I believe that we have much more wisdom and intuition than we think, and by opening ourselves to God we can get in touch with parts of our being that most of us hide or ignore.

## Behind our masks

At an informal gathering I went to recently, a friend was telling us about some of what was happening in her life. It was good news as well as bad news, but my friend said to us, 'Please don't be too nice, or I might burst into tears!' She recognised how fragile she was feeling, and knew that while she was being 'professional' she could cope, but if we were to start to relate to her at a personal level, she would cave in.

It seems a lot of us walk around with our masks firmly in place, and no one would ever know what we are really feeling unless we told them. Even then, half the time they won't believe us unless they have the wisdom to know that even the cheeriest-seeming people can be hiding heavy sadness and pain.

During a telephone conversation with a colleague, I told him how his support and enthusiasm gave me strength. He responded by saying that he took me to be a fairly buoyant person. Ah, yes, I told him, but you have no idea what it takes to be buoyant!

Anyway, most people don't need to know what's going on inside. That's for your one or two very close friends, or those people who come into your life with amazing timing, and are there to help and then move on. I believe God sends certain people when we need them, as God also brings the right books and opportunities into our lives. This is part of what I mean when I say that I try to live 'in the

Spirit'. By opening up ourselves to God's Holy Spirit we can have the faith that we will be in the right place at the right time, and that God will send someone to us when we really need help.

Suffering is a very alienating, exhausting and lonely business. Even if we accept that other people suffer too, no one can know quite how much it hurts at the time. Sometimes I've been glad people can't see what I feel like inside, and at other times I have ached for someone to come up to me and put their arms around me and say, 'Christina, you look so sad. Please know that I love you.' In fact, that is exactly what one friend said to me while I was still grieving after my father died, and it helped to pull me out of my despondency. A simple word, a simple gesture. I wonder if we really have any idea how much we can affect other people's lives with just a few words and a timely hug.

One of the effects my father dying had on me was to make me resolve to tell people how much I love them, and to say, out loud, all the good things that I think about the people I am with. I am sorry to say that I have not lived up to that intention as well as I might have wished, because I have been too concerned about what people will think of me. Will I come across as overly friendly? Will I be seen as a flatterer? Will they think I say those things to everyone?

Over and over again I determine not to listen to these voices, but to act in the way I believe to be right. The more I realise that loving someone is wanting to give as well as to receive, then I can tell myself that, whatever they think of me, if I say what I feel, then I have done what is genuine for me. What they make of it is their business, but usually I find that people are starving for attention, affirmation and compliments. I am sure most people are delighted to be told something nice about themselves. I know how good it makes me feel!

I remember the poster with a picture of a huge ice cream sundae, smothered in whipped cream, with a cherry on top. The caption reads, 'I can live for a month off a good compliment!' I think that's probably true, so perhaps we should be thinking about how we can go around dishing out ice cream sundaes. I'm sure someone you know is hungry for one!

## The ongoing battle

It seems to be universally accepted that, if you focus on the positive and state what you want to have happen, you will help it to come about, while if you repeat the negative and state your fears, you may bring about the very thing you want to avoid. Job is a character in the Old Testament, caught up in a battle between God and Satan. Job was a good man and had a good life before Satan was given free rein to see if he could get Job to curse God. After Satan had destroyed all of Job's livestock and killed his servants and even his children, Job was still loyal to God and did not blame God for his troubles. Even after Job had been covered in oozing sores all over his body, he would still not curse God. But Job was, quite understandably, distraught and near despair. At one stage he curses the day he was born, but still does not curse God.

He goes on to weep and bemoan his blighted life and says, 'For the thing I fear comes upon me, and what I dread befalls me' (Job 3:25). Even Job, whose tale was told about four thousand years ago, could see a relationship between the things he feared and what eventually happened to him. Even though we believe that God does not indulge in bets with Satan, we can sense that there is a spiritual battle going on, and we still need to focus on the positive. As Paul said, 'fill your minds with those things that are good and that deserve praise: things that are true, noble, right, pure, lovely and honourable' (Philippians 4:8). Or, as some people say, GIGO: garbage in, garbage out!

Don't be surprised if breakthroughs are strangely followed by times of depression or difficulty. Your once healthy confidence is knocked and buffeted. The people in your life seem to be in trouble or needing you all at once. You thought you had moved beyond old patterns of thinking and behaving, and yet you feel as if you're back to square one.

In my experience these can all be signs that you are experiencing spiritual warfare, but don't be frightened by that. Remember, the important battle was won two thousand years ago when Jesus stayed faithful, even though it led to his death. We can have faith that Jesus conquered evil and the powers of darkness, and, even though we may not understand all the details, we can know we are spiritually safe. Even though we still have to stand against evil, and often have to take action, immediate or long term, we can be assured that we have the protection of God's Holy Spirit.

Although evil is still in operation, it will come to an end one day. Unfortunately, in the meantime, people still get twisted, frightened, warped and killed. There is still corruption, perversion and all sorts of cruelty and violence. Apart from human weakness or wilfulness, there is also the fluke of earthly life – the random destruction of nature, seen, for example in the earthquake that happened on 26 December 2004, in South East Asia, resulting in the terrifying tsunami that claimed hundreds of thousands of lives. Life on earth carries the risk of great tragedy and, ultimately, we will all die. But in spite of – in the midst of – any danger, we can claim our spiritual protection. We can claim the truth and power of what Jesus accomplished, and we can stand on the truth that evil has no ultimate power over us. If we live close to God, it is as if we are wrapped in an all-encompassing cloak, which nothing that can ultimately destroy us can penetrate. While we still inhabit planet earth, there will be troubles of one kind or another, and we need to learn not to base our confidence and security on what we see happening around us.

Paul wrote what I consider to be one of the strongest affirmations of God's ability to take care of us, no matter what. He asks, somewhat rhetorically, 'If God is for us, who is against us?' and then, 'Who shall separate us from the love of Christ?' (Romans 8:31, 35). Paul goes on to suggest various things that might separate us from Christ's love, but he concludes with a triumphant flourish that 'neither death nor life, nor angels, nor rulers, nor things present, nor things to come, nor powers, nor height, nor depth, nor anything else in all creation, will be able to separate us from the love of God in Christ Jesus our Lord' (Romans 8:38–39). One gets the feeling that he was rather convinced about that!

The apostle John says of evil spirits, 'Little children, you are of God, and have overcome them; for he who is in you is greater than he who is in the world' (1 John 4:4). *He who is in you is greater than he who is in the world.* That is a fantastic statement. When you wake up in the night in a cold sweat, switch on the light and say it out loud. And call on the name of Jesus. There is a real power and protection for anyone who calls on Jesus. I don't pretend to understand all these things, but I do know there is evil; and I know we have protection from it, but we have to place ourselves continually into God's loving protection. No doubt the angels are working overtime on us as well, but we still need to claim protection in Jesus' name.

We might think that the opposite of fear is a feeling of security or safety, but in John's first letter there is an interesting comparison between fear and love. He writes: 'There is no fear in love, but perfect love casts out fear.' If we are filled with love, there will be no room for fear. It is better if we do not focus on the fear, but focus only on the love. Think of yourself being filled to the brim with God's perfect love, surrounded by God's loving arms. No one and nothing can harm you. You are safe because you are trusting in Love. You are not relying on something that might fail. Remember that you have within you all that is necessary for your protection – the love of God. Obviously, try to exercise good judgement and as far as possible steer clear of danger, and the peace of God which passes all understanding keep your hearts and minds in the knowledge and love of God, and of his Son Jesus Christ our Lord; and the blessing of God almighty, the Father, the Son and the Holy Spirit, be among you, and remain with you always.[6]

### When you can't hang on

One of the things we often tell ourselves and each other is to 'hang on in there'. It's an apt phrase most of the time, and implies that we should continue to summon whatever strength we have to endure what we are going through. On the whole, it's good advice. But there are times when it is not possible to hang on in there, when you know that you have nothing left to give. You feel as if you have no reserves of strength on which to call. At that point, even hanging on seems impossible.

At one time in my life I went through sustained testing of my thoughts and beliefs, not so much about God as about myself, and I was emotionally worn out. I had been 'hanging on' for a long time, yet nothing had been resolved. My life felt heavy and my problems imponderable. No matter how much I tried to think things through, I couldn't see any way ahead.

One night as I lay in bed, after I had been trying particularly hard to think my way through the morass, I had an experience that I had never had before. All of a sudden I had a mental image of myself hanging off a bleak rocky cliff, holding on by my fingertips, suspended over a dark void. I could tell that my fingers were slipping and that I wouldn't be able to hold on for much longer. 'I'm slipping, I'm slipping,' I called out in my mind to God. There was no answer, no flicker of response. 'Help,' I cried, 'I'm falling!' Still no answer, no hint of movement to help me.

I could feel my fingers sliding further off the edge of the cliff, and I called out to God in desperation, 'I can't hold on anymore, so you better catch me!' I finally fell away from the cliff and continued to fall for a long time into total darkness. It was absolutely silent, and it felt as if I was falling slowly, almost as if I was drifting down and down into nothingness. I let myself drift for a while, and soon I was fast asleep.

When I woke up the next morning, I could still feel the silence and darkness inside. I was oddly numb, and felt as if I was in a strange, soundless limbo. All I knew was that I had let go. I could function perfectly well on a superficial and practical level, but deep inside I was suspended, waiting.

This state continued for several days, and I didn't know when and if I would ever reach anywhere, or how long I would be in this state of limbo. I had stopped trying to think things through, and I neither worried nor rejoiced. I was unable to feel anything on that level; it was if my internal life was on pause. Then, after about a week, I began to sense something had happened. Something had changed. The only way I can describe it is that I became aware that *I was being held.*

I knew then that I had not vanished or been destroyed. I had neither lost nor damaged my identity. I could not tell exactly what had happened, but I knew beyond any doubt that I was being held in the arms of a loving God. *I* had failed to hang on in there, but that was not the end. Even though I had let go and given up the impossible struggle, God was there. Even though I had let go, God had not gone. All the time, God was there, holding me in his everlasting arms.

My problems did not magically evaporate, but I had gained a new understanding of God's love and presence. Slowly, I was able to see things with fresh eyes, and eventually the way forward became clear. My falling taught me about God's steadfastness. By losing my hold on the edge of the cliff, I discovered myself to be held securely in the arms of the One who is Love.

I am convinced that there is great cause for hope. Even if you have given up on yourself, God has not given up on you. God doesn't give up. God waits with open arms, weeping when we weep, and aching for us to come home. Do not despair of the darkness, because the light will come. Those who draw near to Christ have been given the promise of dawn. Let every morning remind you, that as the sun rises without fail, so God loves you without fail. When everything else has fallen away, Love will still be there. And remember the words of Mother Julian: 'all shall be well, and all shall be well, and all manner of thing shall be well.'

## 7

## *Love in Action*

Whether we know it or like it, other people matter to us. The environmentalists can teach us a thing or two about the inter-relatedness of all of life. What we do with the waste products from our factories affects the purity of our air and water, which in turn affects the health of plants and other creatures under the sea and on land. Cutting down vast swathes of rainforest does not just ruin the habitats of numerous species, it affects the fragile ecosystem of the immediate area, and far beyond. The relative wealth and wasteful-ness of countries in the North affects the prosperity of countries in the global South. We cannot pretend any more that we don't know; we have passed the age of innocence.

The overall purpose and meaning of Jesus' life on earth was to show people who God is and to help them to become vessels and channels of God's love. The new commandment that Jesus gave his followers had a two-way focus: loving God and loving one another. Jesus told his friends that, after he had gone, 'the one who believes in me will also do the works that I do and, in fact, will do greater works than these, because I am going to the Father' (John 14:12). Jesus always intended that his followers carry on his work.

Part of accepting God's love is accepting God's perspective on the people and situations around us. Compassion is looking at others the way God sees them. Jesus saw others this way, and it led him to heal and feed people, cast out evil spirits and raise the dead. It also led him to challenge injustice, speak the truth – and take the consequences. Seeing through the eyes of compassion is not a pas-sive stance; it will lead to action.

Teresa of Avila, a young woman who lived in Spain in the six-teenth century, had a deep understanding of what it meant to be a Christian disciple. After a mystical experience of God, Teresa's life was transformed, and she devoted herself to running and founding convents. She wrote what is usually considered to be a prayer, but I don't see it as a prayer at all. Prayers are directed to God, and this piece of writing is directed to other people: it is more of a charge.

> Christ has no body now on earth but yours;
> yours are the only hands with which he can do his work,
> yours are the only feet with which he can go about the
>     world,
> yours are the only eyes through which his compassion
> can shine forth upon a troubled world.
> Christ has no body now on earth but yours.

A more contemporary Teresa, Mother Teresa of Calcutta, also wrote about this call to service in the name of Christ:

> Love cannot remain by itself – it has no meaning. Love has to be put into action and that action is service. How do we put the love of God in action? By being faithful to our family, to the duties that God has entrusted to us. Whatever form we are, able or disabled, rich or poor, it is not how much we do but how much love we put in the doing, a lifelong sharing of love with others.[1]

For her, love was the all-important ingredient.

If there was a secret as to why she could carry on for so many years serving the sick and dying, it was her underlying view of people. Evidently, over the bath where Mother Teresa and her fellow Sisters of Mercy washed those who had been brought in to their centre, a sign was hung printed with the words, 'The body of Christ'. When she looked into the eyes of destitute and dying people, Mother Teresa said she always saw the eyes of Jesus looking back. She did not see her work as going about performing worthy deeds for the poor: she was washing, feeding and comforting Jesus Christ.

Of course, Mother Teresa wasn't the only one who saw people like that. I meet many so-called ordinary people who are caring for a disabled child, or an ill partner, or an ailing parent. These people go about the business of life, rarely complaining, displaying the type of courage and endurance more commonly associated with military heroes. There are others, so many others, who live their lives with this commitment to love in action in the name of Christ. People who work with drug addicts, victims of torture, prisoners on remand, refugees, lepers, the homeless, the hungry, the mentally ill; the list is very, very long. They are changing the world, even if most of the world doesn't yet know it. Their actions are helping to usher in God's kingdom of love and light.

Archbishop Desmond Tutu, is another who sees the inescapable link between justice and faith. For Tutu, injustice is blasphemy, because it denies the image of God in others. He sees racism and apartheid as examples of this type of blasphemy, the inability to see other people as 'God's stand-ins', as Tutu described it in a sermon he preached during a visit to England in 1995. He said:

> We are made in the image of God, who has a bias to those on the margins of life. So it is holy to leave part of the harvest for those he favours. Sin alienates, splits, divides. Love includes and embraces. 'In as much as you have done it to my sister and my brother you did it to me,' says God: so wherever we tread there is the possibility of the holy, the chance to touch God.

Those who reach out in compassion may discover the 'chance to touch God' in the people they meet. Those who are in great need may not see God unless there is a touch from another human. That is why what Mother Teresa did was so powerful: she touched and held the untouchable. So, too, with Princess Diana; she instinctively reached out to those with the recognition of someone who also suffered. She was filled with empathy and compassion, whether or not she ever knew its source. She was not afraid to touch. The American poet Tim Timmer expresses his own desperate need and near despair in his poem 'Kind Excuse', part of which takes on a bitterly sarcastic tone:

> We are to live groaning:
> Live bleeding.
> Bits and pieces chipped out of our bones.
> The Lord will heal – will mend.
> Will soothe.
> Heaven forbid he uses
> Your arms though.

Heaven forbid he uses your words –
Heaven forbid I see
My Christ in your eyes . . .

Some things require commitment,
don't they?
Run from those like the plague – Right?
How often have we held a box teeming with gauze
bandages
and ointment
but at the sight of one bleeding
given them merely paper words to patch their wounds:
and crawled away,
hoping to avoid another confrontation . . .
We will be held accountable,
for the infections we caused.
by not wanting to use
what God has given to us,
leaving other's incisions to scar up . . .
You choose to rest upon hearty excuses,
and never may see
you hold a remedy in your hand.

Where there is talk and no action, words ring hollow. Where there is action, words are hardly needed. The love of Christ *can* heal us, but it usually has to be administered through another human being. Most of us can only see Christ in other people when we feel the love of another. Some people can only ever begin to see God in their lives if they see us first. As John Tinsley, the former Bishop of Bristol once said, 'You and I are set to be nothing less than disclosures of God to other people.'[2]

Of course, we can also know Christ through nature, or music, or silence, or with animals. For me, these things are closely tied to joy, but most hurts and wounds, at some stage, require the healing touch of another human being. If there is no one to do that for us, our initial wound is made worse by a sense of isolation and alienation.

Nigel Goodwin, a man who travels the world reaching out with the love of Christ to people in the arts, talks about the 'violence' of not being loved, of never being touched lovingly, of not being noticed. He reminds me, as have so many others who have seen and experienced deep hurt, that we are meant to be in relationships. We are not meant to be 'doing life' on our own.

The American theologian Tom Sine challenges the way we in the West order our lives. In his latest book *Mustard Seed vs McWorld*, Sine suggests new designs for housing so that several families can share certain communal facilities – and the mortgage. He encourages people to meet together with friends more often, in an informal way, to share meals and laughter. He thinks we should talk more about what has mattered to us recently, and give thanks for it. He urges us to celebrate, have more parties, take the time to get to know other people, show we care, and have more fun! We need to rediscover the joy of being alive.

There is a parable in the New Testament about a time in the future when Christ will judge all the people who have ever lived. Christ separates them into two groups. The unrighteous people are placed at Christ's left hand, and the righteous at his right hand, the position of honour. Christ says to those on his right, 'Come, you that are blessed by my Father! Come and possess the kingdom which has been prepared for you ever since the creation of the world. I was hungry and you fed me, thirsty and you gave me a drink; I was a stranger and you received me in your homes, naked and you clothed me; I was sick and you took care of me, in prison and you visited me.' Then the righteous people ask when it was that they did any of these kind things for Christ. The answer comes: 'I tell you, whenever you did this for one of the least important of these brothers of mine, you did it for me.'

The unrighteous group is then ordered away into the eternal fire because they did not care for Christ. They also ask when it was that they had had the opportunity to show, or not to show, Christ any kindness. They are told, 'I tell you, whenever you refused to help one of these least important ones, you refused to help me' (from Matthew 25:31–44).

The message is clear: how we treat other people is how we are treating God. God lives in the people he has created, and we are to approach each other with that understanding. I was told as a child that when I met someone who frightened me or whom I did not like, I was to pray a silent prayer: 'May the Christ in me see the Christ in you.' Allow God's Spirit in you to reach out to touch God's Spirit in the other.

If only we really believed that each and every person was made in the image of God, we could, hopefully, create a more just and merciful world. The opponent, the outsider and the oddity: these too carry God within. These too have the capacity to respond to God. If they do not choose God, that is their decision, but woe to me if I prevent them from seeing God or pervert the message of God's love and forgiveness. We should at least be more prepared to give people a chance. Remember, after all, that by welcoming the stranger, some 'have entertained angels unawares' (Hebrews 13:2).

I believe we can only challenge others from a position of personal commitment. If it is to make a real, lasting change, my commitment to what I do must be based on my understanding of God's will. If I don't live it myself, I won't convince you that it's worthwhile, or even desirable. If I don't live it, maybe I don't really believe it.

There are so many areas in life that need Christ's reconciling love and a new understanding of God's vision. The crippling evils of racism, sexism, ageism, and other forms of prejudice and hatred, can only be countered and transformed when we see others the way God sees them.

## Racism

Not many years ago, a young man was beaten and stabbed to death because of the colour of his skin. His murderers have still not been brought to justice. Stephen Lawrence has been only one of many killed in racist murders, but his senseless and violent death, and the courage of his parents, captured both hearts and headlines in a special way.

At a recent meeting of the General Synod of the Church of England in York, John Sentamu, then Bishop of Stepney, presented a report about the Stephen Lawrence Inquiry. Bishop John, one of the very few black bishops in the Church of England, had become involved in the inquiry on behalf of the Lawrence family. He arrived at Synod the night before his presentation. As I was walking through the room where he was preparing for his talk, he and I saw each other and greeted each other warmly. John then introduced me to Neville, a friend standing next to him.

It was only when we shook hands that I suddenly recognised him as Stephen's father. I had no idea what effect he would have on me, but as I hurried on to my next meeting I was overcome with grief. No longer was he just a face on my television screen, a bereaved parent, a man tackling the system. He was a real person who had lost his real son. What also hit me with fresh force was the reality of the hatred and prejudice that had killed his son.

My first memory of racism was when I was a child, living in the Bahamas. At that time my family was living on a tiny island called Deep Water Cay. We were the only white people who lived there. Others came to fish at the club my parents ran, which was staffed by Bahamians from the nearby island; the women worked in the kitchen and tidied the guestrooms, and the men piloted the boats while out fishing with the guests.

We got on well with our Bahamian friends, sharing a deep friendship based on mutual respect, genuine affection and the knowledge that we were brothers and sisters in Christ. We also shared a certain solidarity that came from living in a remote place, and being at the mercy of storms and other dangers. Life could be tough and we were all in it together.

One week, a man came to fish on the island, an old-fashioned man from the Deep South in the United States. At that time my mother's sister, Jan Payne, and her husband John were visiting us for a while. They, like my parents, were deeply committed Christians, confident, gentle and unshakeable. I don't remember the details, but, after hours of speaking with my aunt and uncle and my parents, the man from the South became a Christian. His was a dramatic conversion; he was filled with love and he overflowed with tears. Evidently, all his life this man had been steeped in racist prejudice and hatred. Up till then, his oath, which he had proudly kept, had been that he would never shake hands with a black man. As he opened his heart to God, God opened his heart to his fellow human beings. For the next few days until he left, this man was to be seen, grinning, weeping freely and hugging everyone. The man who had boasted that he would never shake hands with a black man, was now hugging and being hugged by both the black men and women.

He now saw people with God's eyes, and he was completely changed: it was as if he was a different person. Only God's radical love could have changed that man, and only God's radical love can change any of us.

## Sexism

On the night I met Neville Lawrence, I had to hurry to another meeting, a group of women and men who are working for equality among the sexes in the Church of England. I had been asked to bring an update from National WATCH (Women And The Church). I had managed to stop crying and dry my eyes, but I still was overcome by grief for Stephen Lawrence and his family. I remember thinking that just as racism is real, so too is sexism, otherwise why would we all be gathered in an uncomfortable room at nearly eleven o'clock at night after a long day of Synod business?

As I looked around the room I saw some women who had become ordained after years of waiting. I spotted others, women and men, who had given years of their lives to work for the ordination of women. Here they were, still in the Church, still gracious and loving, and still working to help bring about a vision of the Church as a place where men and women are valued equally.

I had never planned on becoming so involved in these issues, but, years earlier, the more I had thought about my faith, and the more I had thought about the situation in the Church, the more I became convinced that God made no value judgement between the sexes. There are obvious differences, to be sure, but one sex is not somehow more useful to God or closer to God than the other. We are all human beings, together created in the image of God.

In 1992, as the Church of England was preparing for the decisive vote on women priests, I started working for the Movement for the Ordination of Women. This was not a planned career move, but I was sure I had been called to this work. Over the years, some well-meaning people have asked me, their voices just above a whisper, how much longer I plan on being involved with the 'women's' issues. I tell them I don't know; I suppose as long as I feel God is calling me to remain involved. Inwardly, I smile. Asking me that is like asking someone from South Africa how much longer they will bother with getting rid of the legacy of apartheid and creating a just society. As long as it takes? For the rest of my life? Until all are equally valued? Until God calls me to something different?

My concern for the 'women's' issues is a concern for the Church as the whole people of God, women and men together, living as the Body of Christ. It is not a case of 'jobs for the girls' or any other trendy, or even worthy, concept. It is a longing for the Church to mirror the radical equality and mutual love, respect and interdependence of the Trinity. It is a longing to recognise and to live out the consequences of seeing that it is humanity as a whole that was made in the image of God, not just males or females on their own.

Often, I have to explain to slightly worried people that I am not interested in replacing the present patriarchy with a matriarchy. Rather, I, and the thousands of others who share these views, are interested in the Church becoming what God wants us to be, freed from the prejudices of the past, and free to bring and to be the Good News of Jesus Christ. The goal is to help 'everyone in the Church to become the community of people by which the Kingdom of God is established on earth'.[3]

Why then, to stay on this subject a moment longer, is there still opposition to women taking their place alongside men in the ministry of the Church? Where is there still confusion about what is 'permissible' for women? Why is there still so much prejudice against women in the churches and in our society?

To answer these questions is to trace a flawed and at times tragic legacy through the centuries, a legacy that has been influenced by Greek philosophical thought as well as by ancient Hebrew reactions to Babylonian legends. It is a journey that winds its way through scientific and medical breakthroughs, discoveries that changed the future of thought and belief. It is to travel in time to countries and cultures that are so different from ours that we cannot even fully appreciate the differences. It is to learn how to hold on to the eternal truth of the Bible and guard its message of God's liberating love, while discerning what is time- and culture-bound, and now needs to be viewed in a different light.

In fact, I see part of my identity as a minor traveller on this voyage of discovery, someone who is trying to piece together why it is that there is such resistance to accepting that women, as much as men, are made in the image of God, and why it is that women are still regarded as unable to express and embody the presence of the risen Christ.

We need to grow to the stage where we can acknowledge that men do not exist in isolation from women any more than women exist in isolation from men. We need to see both sexes and our gender identities as existing in relation to the other and of having equal value. There must be space and opportunity for expression and discovery of the other. Though for the vast majority of people our sex is a given at birth, our gender roles are more fluid. All cultures recognise gender differences between the sexes, but they are different for different cultures. It's fair to say that gender roles are largely socially determined.

The goal is not to erase and ignore the differences between men and women, but rather to see how we can interact in the most loving and creative ways. Our bodies and our sex determine some basic ways in which we experience life, and we need to listen carefully, to one another and to God, if we are to bring God's liberating and transforming power into our lives. As the theologian Miroslav Volf observes, 'clearly, when half of the human race (women) is consistently deemed inferior and frequently mistreated, we have a problem of major proportions'.[4]

Racism and sexism are only two areas of injustice. The American preacher Tony Campolo tells the story of when he was in high school, he and his friends used to taunt Roger, a fellow student, who was effeminate. One day Tony's friends grabbed Roger and threw him into a shower cubicle and urinated on him. Tony did not take part, but his friends told him what they had done. Later that day, Roger went home and killed himself. When Tony heard, he was overcome with guilt and wished that he had gone to comfort Roger. But it was too late.

Homophobia, poverty, pollution, torture, international debt, female genital mutilation, human trafficking, corruption, hard-core pornography: the list is long and ugly, and there is not space here to look at it in more detail. Should we bother to take a stand? Can we make a difference? I actually don't think those are the right questions. I think there is one question above all others that we must ask, and that is: what light does the crucified and risen Christ throw on these areas?

When brought into his sphere of love and justice, how do these things look? If there is dissonance with what the cross and the resurrection show us, then we must act. It is not an option, a hobby for an idle moment, but an imperative, if we are ever to usher in the kingdom of peace on earth. We can't all be on the front line, but we can support those who are, with our time, talents, money and prayers. Whatever else we do, we can all help to challenge prejudice and ignorance in how we live our lives.

I end this chapter with a blessing from Canada, by an unknown author, given to me by the Reverend June Maffin from Vancouver.

May God bless you with discomfort at easy answers,
half-truths, superficial relationships,
so that you will live deep within your heart.

May God bless you with anger at injustice,
oppression and exploitation of people,
so that you will work for justice, equity and peace.

May God bless you with tears to shed for those who suffer
from pain,
rejection, starvation and war,
so that you will reach out your hand to comfort them and
change their pain to joy.

May God bless you with the foolishness
to think that you can make a difference in the world,
so that you will do the things which others tell you cannot
be done.

## 8

## *When God Calls*

For most of the time, my sense of being called has unfolded gradually as I live out my life, but there have also been moments of insight and peculiar vision. Let me go back a few years. I did my undergraduate degree at Pomona College, a liberal arts college in California and one of the Claremont cluster of colleges. It was a four-year, full-time course. Towards the end of my first year, I began to take a great interest in African dance and poetry. One thing led to another, and I finally arranged to spend the first half of the next academic year in Natal, studying indigenous South African dance forms, while earning my keep teaching and helping out at a Christian mission. I felt very excited about my plans, and I was confident that God had blessed my preparations.

However, one small obstacle presented itself: my visa had not come by the time I was due to leave, and I was eager to be on my way. I came up with a bright idea! My flight was scheduled to stop in London and, what was more, at that time my sister Robin was on the Isle of Wight, preparing for Cowes Week. She had studied for, and passed, her captain's licence and was spending a few years sailing in cross-Atlantic races and other yachting events. Why not fly to London, pick up my visa there, visit Robin and then fly on to South Africa?

So, I left America with only one suitcase and a small shoulder bag. I reasoned that I would only be in England for a few days, so I packed a few changes of clothing in my carry-on bag. When I arrived at Heathrow, I checked my suitcase in a locker, and travelled in to London to collect my visa from the South African embassy in Trafalgar Square.

My visa had not arrived. Not unduly bothered, I travelled to the Isle of Wight and met up with Robin. It was great to see her and talk about her sailing plans and meet some of her fellow crewmates. We had only a couple of days together, and then she set sail. I returned to London. Still no visa. Only now, it was no visa and no place to stay.

In Cowes, Robin and I had stayed together in a small guesthouse, and after she left I had gone back to the room to collect my things. As I was packing, I noticed that Robin had left a small notepad behind. I was worried that it might contain valuable information which she would need, but after flicking through it I only found a few 'to do' lists and an address and telephone number in London that our aunt, Jan Payne, had given her, should she have had the time to travel in England.

The scribbled address, not even intended for me, was the only lead I had. My budget certainly didn't include nights at the Ritz! I rang the number and was greeted down the phone by a man who could not have been more kind. Of course I must come and stay with him!

It will just be for the one night I told him, confident that the next day my visa would come. My visa didn't come the next day, nor the day after that. In fact, it never came. But it took another two months before I gave up on my plans of going to South Africa. During that time I stayed for over a fortnight with my new friend Douglas Evans. Then he found me a flat to share with three delight-ful and generous women. They were wonderful to me. One of them, Roseanne Dill, took me with her when she visited a cousin in Shropshire, where I got to ride on a combine harvester for the first time. Another, Diana Ridler, introduced me to the rest of her family, who made me feel like an honoured guest. There were lunches at their cricket club, dinners at their home, and Diana's brother Charles took me under his wing, which involved frequent-ing a pub called the Zetland, where I tried my first Guinness.

They could not have been kinder, but their flat was intended for three, and I made four. Besides, they had said they could have me for only a few weeks, which was generous enough – not a few months! So, next I moved in with a man named Christopher, from their church, who was, I discovered, passionate about justice issues, particularly poverty. He lived on tea and digestive biscuits, as did I when I stayed with him.

After a few more weeks, I was told by a clerk at the embassy, who had taken pity on me, that my visa had been denied. At this time, apartheid was still in force, and by indicating on my application that I was interested in black South African art forms, I had aroused the suspicions of the officials. They refused to believe that I was only a student, and so I became a *persona non grata* in South Africa.

I went back to America with a confused mixture of feelings. I was so glad to have met all the wonderful people I stayed with, and to have had two carefree months in London, but I was devastated about not getting to South Africa. The biggest issue by far was to do with my faith: if I had heard God wrong about South Africa, what else was I hearing wrong? Had I heard God correctly in the first place? If so, why had this happened? My confidence was knocked, and I doubted all the ideas I had had about my future. What if they were all misguided? What was I really supposed to be doing?

Only years later, with the benefit of hindsight, have I been able to accept what happened that summer, and to make some sense of it. What if, I now ask myself, it was never about getting to South Africa? Would I have really wanted to go there at that time anyway? What if it was a gift – a gift of a few months in the country that was later to become my home? What if it was so that I could feel comfortable about the thought of living in England?

What does it mean to be called by God? Is everyone called, or is it just for the chosen few? According to Paul, all Christians are called, 'to live a life worthy of the calling to which you have been called, with all humility and gentleness, with patience, bearing with one another in love, making every effort to maintain the unity of the Spirit in the bond of peace' (Ephesians 4:1–3).

Some do have special calls, such as to become ordained, or to work in a certain country, or to take up a specific career. My GP, Peter Gough, was motivated to study medicine as a result of his belief in God. He wanted to help people in a practical way, and felt called to become a doctor. Within the last few years his concern for the welfare of other people prompted him to start up a charity called Khandelight, which supports health and development projects in Rajasthan. Peter and his impressively active committee have raised many thousands of pounds for some of the poorest of the poor people in Rajasthan, and in particular girls and women, who suffer special discrimination and deprivation. Now every year hundreds of women are helped to become literate and given basic health training. Khandelight also makes it possible for people to have drinking water, water to grow crops, better housing and much more. One man's vision has given self-esteem, health and a better life to thousands of people.

Some of my ordained friends can trace their calling back to when they were children. Canon Flora Winfield had a difficult childhood, but it was in that 'desperate experience of loneliness and alienation' that her sense of vocation began. At about the age of nine, Flora remembers being overwhelmed by a sense of love, and later, in her teens, she became aware that her understanding of other peoples' pain would somehow be 'required' of her. She reflects:

> For me, the experience of vocation has been about weakness — and it has always felt as if that which is most broken in me is that which is most called. And what is called is not only what is saved from the wreckage, what survives and flourishes and grows towards the light, but what remains broken, is unmendable, but is most profoundly touched by God.'[1]

Others have been called later in life, when the call has required a dramatic change in their lives. Jane Bass was driving home one day when she heard a quiet voice say, 'I want you to be a priest.' Jane later wrote about the experience: 'I was nearly paralysed with shock and pulled into the nearest coffee shop for a stiff black coffee and to consider what manner of request this was or whether I had gone dotty in the hot sun.'[2]

For most people, however, the calling of God seems to be breathed into their lives as their lives unfold. They are drawn to certain things at certain times, and the necessary doors swing open. They rarely know exactly what they are meant to achieve, but they often have the sense that they are where they should be.

I can best describe my own sense of calling as a sense of *obedience*. I am aware that I can obey God, or not, and if I were to abandon what I am doing, or even change the focus, I would feel as if I were disobeying God. I'd like to be able to say that, as a result of my calling, I am filled with inner peace and fortitude at all times — but that just isn't the case. Sometimes, the positive, feel-good factor is completely absent, and all I have to go on is this sense of obedience, that I am following where someone else is guiding.

Often, it's a case of wondering how thick the clouds are at any given time. Glimpses of blue sky, when I can see clearly where I am going, are nice, but not necessary. Corrie Ten Boom used to say that we needed a ticket only when we were ready to board the train, and not before. Being called gives purpose, vision and strength, but not always an overall or detailed view of how things will unfold.

I have mentioned that obedience is part of responding to God's call, and that's true, but it's not like a cut-and-dried military exercise. It's not as if we have to jump to attention when the divine command is boomed out on a loudspeaker. Part of the good news of Jesus Christ is being set free from rules, and not having to prove that we are good enough. We are not meant to live in slavish obedience to the old, written law, but in the freedom of God's Spirit. It's about having the impossible burden of getting life 'right' replaced with an invitation to follow the Lord of love. We also need to remember that we live by God's grace, not by earning spiritual brownie points.

And yet, when I look deeply at what the way of love means, sometimes it seems as if I'm back with a myriad of rules and regulations, a whole array of 'thou shalt nots'. This is one of the paradoxes of living a life of faith. We accept our freedom in Christ, and then we discover that the love of Christ keeps us from sinning more effectively than any list of rules!

When I was a teenager, I didn't trust either myself or God enough to live by the rule of love. I piled on extra rules so that I could feel safe. I read the Bible, which is, of course, good. I went to prayer meetings and house groups, which are also good. I read additional devotional material, and I fasted – all good things. I consciously tried to live a very pure and holy life.

After several years of living like this, I realised that I still could not control all my actions and words, and certainly not my thoughts. I also made the mistake of confusing my basic human needs and desires, as well as strong temptations, with sin itself. Just having impure thoughts made me feel guilty, and in response to my imperfection, I pushed myself even harder.

Looking back, I think I fell into the trap of thinking that I really could earn spiritual Brownie points and win God's affection. If only

I could banish all stray thoughts, unholy desires and momentary lapses of righteousness, I thought, then God would see how good I am and how hard I'm trying and . . . and what? What was I expecting of God? What was I doing it for?

I thought that my focus was on God, but I realised that I had really been much more concerned with myself: how was *I* doing, how was *I* measuring up as a Christian?

By trying to be the best Christian on earth, I had created for myself my own unholy rat race, my own criteria of how good I was, and I was withholding my own acceptance and praise from myself whenever I felt I didn't come up to the mark. Since hardly a day ever went by without my failing in some way, you can imagine that I had got onto a very harsh treadmill indeed. The only answer seemed to be to keep trying harder and harder.

Or get off. Somewhere along the line, I realised that I would burn out if I carried on the way I was going. Friends were particularly helpful, some because they understood, and others simply because they could tell that something was wrong.

One close friend tried to tell me that I didn't have to *strive*, that being a Christian was letting God love me and lead me. Thanks to her, I began to recognise my unhealthy drive for perfection and question whether it was what God was really calling me to. Other friends, some not even sharing my Christian faith, cared enough about me to ask things like, 'Why are you so rigid? Why don't you loosen up a bit?'

At the time I flatly denied I was rigid or that I needed to loosen up at all. Of course, my very reaction would have confirmed to them just what state I was in. But I could not see it myself. I was living life to the best of my ability, and I was glad that I was avoiding the more spectacular types of sin. But, increasingly, I knew I wasn't happy, and I couldn't imagine living at this level of control over myself for years and years to come. For all my brave effort, I still fought with errant thoughts and other pangs of envy, resentment and fear. This combination of extreme self-discipline and the suppression of my natural human desires had fermented into an unlovely and contradictory potion of self-loathing and self-righteousness.

At one and the same time I considered myself to be doing better than everyone else I knew, keeping more pure and sinless, and yet I was all too aware of the unlovely thoughts and impulses I still had. I began to envy people who could accept themselves for who they were and who didn't seem to set themselves impossible standards. I marvelled that some of my friends could fall off the 'narrow' way and still not berate themselves. They, unlike me, seemed to be able to acknowledge what they had done, and almost shrug it off with an, 'Oh well, you win some, you lose some' attitude. Secretly, I wished I could feel the same about my faults and failings, but I still prided myself, like the Pharisee in the Bible, that 'I was not as one of these.' *I* was much stronger, more disciplined, more in control, but my superficial so-called perfection had become a darker sin than all the sins and wrongdoings of all my friends. I felt utterly trapped by my predicament. How could I be living such a righteous life and yet be so miserable? If I was doing so well, why did I feel like the biggest failure around?

It's easy to see now that it was because I could not accept God's love for me, but at the time I didn't know what I was doing wrong. I could not even accept God's love when I knew I had done something worthy, because I was so conscious of the seething turmoil of my inner thoughts. I gained a small amount of reassurance from a familiar sounding plea by Paul: 'I do not understand my own actions. For I do not do what I want, but I do the very thing I hate . . . Wretched man that I am!' (Romans 7:15, 24). Paul doesn't stop there, but goes on to write one of the most powerful declarations of personal liberation: 'There is therefore now no condemnation for those who are in Christ Jesus. For the law of the Spirit of life in Christ Jesus has set me free from the law of sin and death.'

The liberating truth contained in those two sentences explodes the heresy that we have to grovel perpetually and apologise continually in order to be considered acceptable to God. If we are in Christ Jesus, that is, if we believe in Jesus and have asked him to give us another chance, then all that is in the past has been wiped clean and we come to God free and forgiven. And not only forgiven: if we are in Christ we are 'a new creation; the old has passed away, behold, the new has come' (2 Corinthians 5:17). Eventually, I learned to 'lighten up' and it was easier for me to accept that I was loved and free to follow God's Spirit.

## A meandering path

With any sense of being called, there is an element of timing. Sometimes I believe we are given a vision of what will happen later in our lives. In our enthusiasm we try to make it happen *now*. When it doesn't work, we give up and say that we must have got the wrong impression about what God was saying to us. We forget that God lives outside of time, and that for God one day is as a thousand. We do not trust that if God has given us a vision, God will help to bring it to pass.

When I graduated I wasn't sure which direction to take. There were so many things I liked to do, and I couldn't make up my mind which one to pick first (I guess I've had this problem at many stages in my life). I had no idea even how to get started with most of my dreams. Eventually, after four years in California, I decided to go back east and start my quest for my path in life there. I found a room to share with my artist friend Chrisi Anderson, in an old actor's club called The Lamb's Club, in New York City, right off Times Square. I began the hunt for a job that would combine my love of the arts and God. In the end, I took a job as a secretary in a branch of Columbia Pictures.

Screen Gems made television ads and produced one of the longest-running American soap operas, called *The Edge of Night*. During my interview, I was open about my ultimate ambitions, namely, to become involved with the creative side of programming, and the person who hired me assured me that I would soon be given extra experience in those areas.

In the meantime, I typed out running schedules for the week's work, and I welcomed visitors to the company. It wasn't long, however, before I had been given a tiny, non-speaking part in *The Edge of Night*, and I was also asked to act in a promotional video for a new Oil of Ulay ad campaign. The promo was for the French market, and I was chosen at the last minute because the actress that had been scheduled couldn't speak, or even pronounce, French!

I remember being hauled away from my desk in a great panic, and having to learn the script while my make-up was being applied. Evidently, the video did the trick, and the French bought into the ad campaign. I really thought this might be the beginning of a new career. People could see my talent, and in no time, I reasoned, I'd be involved in making intelligent, meaningful television, both in front of the camera and behind the scenes.

After nearly a year, however, nothing more had happened. I had pushed at certain doors, met with suggested people, and yet – nothing. Also during this time I was getting angry. Every day I had to walk across town, from Times Square to the east side, and every day I had to withstand the constant barrage of lecherous looks, comments and sounds from some of the men I passed. These encounters were different from the brazen wolf whistles of the building-site workers, or the occasional cheeky, but harmless, comment. What started to eat into me and upset me was a much more subtle manner from certain men. They never touched me, but it was as if they used me for their own enjoyment. Little gestures, such as sticking their tongues out, or licking their lips, or just staring intently at various parts of my anatomy, started to unsettle me. I dressed modestly anyway, but I went out of my way to cover up. They made obscene low sounds as I passed on the pavement, and I found myself resenting this more and more. After nearly a year of this treatment, a caldron of anger was bubbling away inside me.

Many mornings on the way to work I would step into a church that was on my route, and enter another world, a world that helped me to cope. It was a huge, cavernous church, with stained-glass windows and the beautiful, calming scent of incense. It reminded me of the hundreds of churches I had visited with my family the year we travelled through Europe. Here was sanctuary, peace, holiness, a moment of escape. I would walk through the heavy door and leave the obscenities behind me.

Almost immediately there would be tears in my eyes, and I would sink into a chair, or light a candle, and take deep breaths and try not to cry out loud. God seemed so far from the streets, so absent from my daily walk. Even though the actor's club I lived in had been bought by a group of Christians, it didn't provide this type of sanctuary. It had a thriving ministry to the acting community, particularly the seedier elements, and to the down and outs, as well as the pimps and prostitutes around Times Square. Most of the people involved in the church were actors, singers and dancers themselves, and services were a wonderful combination of excellent worship and powerful compelling performance. I saw many lives changed, and knew many people who were rescued from lives of drug and drink dependence, debauchery and general despair. I took part in some of the church performances, and for a time I even became part of a puppet street theatre troupe. It was a challenging and amazing ministry, and made the basic living standards easier to accept. I saw a purpose for living there. But what it couldn't offer was what I found in this dark, quiet, incense-filled church.

In here, I was able to let down, take the happy cheery mask from my face and collapse for a few brief moments, acknowledging how alone, unhappy and desperate I was feeling. No one at the club where I lived or at work had guessed how I was really feeling, and I didn't even let my parents know when I would go out on Long Island to visit them. After all, I wanted my first year launched into the big bad world to be a raving success. I wasn't supposed to be miserable. I was supposed to be having the time of my life. The world was supposed to be my oyster. My roommate Chrisi knew a bit, but I hid the extent of my unhappiness even from her.

And so, for a few minutes in the mornings when I wasn't running late, I would soak in the timeless peace and let myself be filled with the familiar scents and sights and sounds. Some mornings I would join the group of silent people taking communion, and file slowly past the priests, taking the sacrament they offered. At some point I realised that this was a Roman Catholic Church, and I didn't know whether or not I, an Anglican, should be taking communion, but no one ever spoke to me and asked me where I came from. Besides, I knew God wouldn't mind, and I certainly didn't mind. To me it was heaven, and I was so grateful that there was this beautiful place right on the way to work.

By the end of the year at Screen Gems, I realised that I could stay there for ever yet never get to do the types of things I wanted to do. I also realised that, fun as soap operas and advertisements were, they were not what I wanted to be doing. So what if I'd had ridden in a lift alone with Woody Allen (neither of us spoke)? So what that I'd been wined and dined and taken to all the best galleries and parties by one of the Screen Gem bosses. I had realised fairly soon that it was because he wanted to humiliate his ex-wife. My time of feeling flattered ended.

## Being given a vision

I went back to stay for a long weekend with my parents, and while I was at home I had an extraordinary experience. I had stretched out on my bed and shut my eyes for a quick nap, but instead of drifting off to sleep I immediately began to see pictures in my mind of various well-known women. Oddly, all the women I 'saw' were from England and the Continent, and yet there I was, on Long Island in America. They were the leaders and trendsetters of their day. As I observed these women passing through my consciousness, I had a strong sense that I would be with them at some point in my life, talking with them, working with them and influencing them with the message of Christ.

This experience lasted only a few minutes, and when it had faded I was filled with an overwhelming sense of purpose and direction, which in turn filled me with elation. I ran to get my mother, and told her about what I had seen. She did not think I was mad, nor did she think it was insignificant. Like me, she accepted it as a glimpse into my future, and we both thanked God for showing me, even briefly, at least a part of what lay ahead.

At that time I could not possibly have known that two years later I would end up marrying an Englishman and living in England. My vision puzzled me at the time, but I accepted the whole experience as a gift from God. I imagined that it was a hint of a far-distant time. I had no idea that it was a preview of a process that would begin so soon.

For a while after that, to my shame, I forgot all about the vision. Instead of trying to charge ahead and bring it to pass, I only thought about it briefly and then let it drift out of my mind. It came back to me about five years later when I had already had my two daughters, Angela and Alex. Along with the fascination and delight of being a parent of two beautiful children, it was also a time of great frustration and loss of direction. I spent most of my time bringing up the family and running a home, with little support. Chris was going through a particularly busy patch, one of the many he has been through, and we had not long moved to a new home.

I had made friends in the village, which proved to be an open and welcoming place, in particular with the Smith family who had moved next door only six months after we arrived. Phil and Sarah's little boy, Ben, was a few months older than Angela, and Sarah was pregnant with their second child, Hannah, who was almost exactly one year younger than Alex. Then, a year after that, our other nextdoor neighbours, John and Tina Curtis, produced a daughter, another Alex. So, up our tiny lane, away from traffic, our three houses and gardens became an open playground for the five children.

It worked a bit like a loose community: we took care of each other's children, and fed and bathed them as was easiest. Without those close friends, I would have been much, much lonelier. My mother-in-law, Margaret Rees, also came over fairly frequently, and usually stayed for a couple of days, bringing handmade dresses and little gifts for the girls. Her staying with us made it possible for me to travel to London, see friends and even go further afield.

Underlying this time, however, was a feeling that I had abandoned any sense of calling, other than that to motherhood, I had ever had. I simply could not see the way forward beyond being constantly with my children. It was probably best that I temporarily lost sight of the vision, because it would have felt like rubbing salt into an open wound. It was all I could do to care for my children and be there for my husband. My world had, more or less, shrunk to the size of our village, the shops in the nearby town and an occasional outing to the local zoo! However, when I was ready to start on the vision, I remembered.

Events unfolded, opportunities came looking for me and, without knowing it, I was beginning to realise the vision. Years on, I am still realising the vision, and I have the strong sense that there is still much to be accomplished, but I am certainly on the way. There has been no sense of arrival, just the sense of knowing myself to be on the right path. I have no idea where the path will continue to lead, only the confidence in the One who is leading. It's risky, it feels uncertain and I don't get to see any maps of where I'm heading, but on the good days it's great! No, on the good days it's fantastic! At long last I am learning to trust: life, myself and God. It has been said that the one who is called is the one that can endure!

Have you ever had a strong urge to study a certain subject? Have you ever fallen completely in love with some new activity, such as playing a musical instrument or dancing? Are you passionate about dogs, or old people, or broadcasting, or biology? I think it's always worthwhile pursuing your deeply felt interests and seeing where they lead you. I know I may have taken a while to discover my chosen path, but then that's because I used to find it difficult to make up my mind. What's more, I was greedy: I wanted to do everything! Listen carefully to what your heart is saying, for it may be whispering where you are to take your next step. Enjoy the process as best you can, trusting that God is always holding you and helping you to become all that you are created to be.

I believe that God can use all our hopes, longings, desires, talents, experiences and thoughts to help establish his kingdom of love. Along the way, inevitably we will sin and stray and fall. We can learn from our mistakes, but we shouldn't go out looking for the brick walls to run into! What I *do* believe is that God can teach us wisdom and obedience through those failures, mistakes and, yes, even the times we deliberately go our own way. If, overall, we are trying to live as Christ would have us do, then everything in our lives can be used to refine and purify us and bring us closer to God.

I know there are times when the Holy Spirit asks me to do something definite and specific, such as pick up the phone or write a letter. I can say 'no', but hopefully I will say 'yes', knowing that every time I say 'yes' I am doing the work of Christ. The course of our lives can be shaped and changed by our responses to God's calling. Every time we hear correctly and obey, we become more completely ourselves, and, I believe, we become more like Christ. Every time we disobey, we stay trapped in ways of being and behaving which do not help us to become all that we can be, nor does it further God's will. When we disobey, the veil comes down again and we become slightly deaf. *Eh, God, was that you? Nah, it couldn't have been.* We turn up the volume of our competing sounds and tune into the noise we prefer.

In *Mere Christianity*, C. S. Lewis writes:

> Every time you make a choice you are turning the central part of you, the part of you that chooses, into something a little different from what it was before. And taking your life as a whole, with all your innumerable choices, all your life long you are slowly turning this central thing into a Heaven creature or into a hellish creature: either into a creature that is in harmony with God, and with other creatures, and with itself, or else into one that is in

a state of war and hatred with God, and with its fellow creatures, and with itself. To be the one kind of creature is Heaven: that is, it is joy, and peace, and knowledge, and power. To be the other means madness, horror, idiocy, rage, impotence, and eternal loneliness. Each of us at each moment is progressing to the one state or the other.[3]

Bishop John V. Taylor also thought that we are creating our ultimate futures with every decision we make. He wrote that when he died he expected to be

confronted with the whole of reality in one impact, streaming towards me. At that moment I am either suddenly going to find it in myself to spread my arms, say yes, and jump into the stream; or else I am going to shrink back and say no. I think all the little decisions I am making here in this short life are the decisions as to whether I will ultimately say yes to reality, or whether I will shut myself up in fear and say no – either preparing me for that big yes, or turning me into the kind of person who will finally shrink into nothing.[4]

Hearing and responding to God's call starts now, and where it ends God only knows. But do we trust? Are we preparing for the big 'yes', or are we living in such a way that we will shrink away into nothingness? Do we have the courage to become something we are not already? Can we stand firm on our faith in a loving God, while sitting lightly to the exact ways and means by which God will reveal his love to us or to anyone else? Can we live with the tension that, as we grow closer to the heart of God, other things around us will seem less important?

I am not advocating that we develop some vague, amorphous spiritual awareness, or an attempt to rise above all human needs and longings. The goal of the saying 'yes', letting go, the trust, the sitting lightly, is always deeper oneness with God. As Madeleine L'Engle says:

For the easterner the goal is *nirvana*, which means 'where there is no wind,' and for us the wind of the Spirit is vital, even when it blows harshly. We do not move from meditation into contemplation, into self-annihilation, into

> death, in order to be freed from the intolerable wheel of
> life. No. We move – are moved – into death in order to
> be discovered, to be loved into truer life by our Maker.[5]

Having to die in order to live may not make sense to everyone,
but it will make sense to everyone who has ever had to give up
cherished hopes and dreams, only to have them return later,
refined, more realistic and at exactly the right time. Sometimes the
dreams don't come back, but others do, dreams you could not have
imagined before. For some, the biggest death will be to their own
sense of being in control; for others it will mean death to a certain
view of yourself that has no part in the reality of God's love. But all
the deaths and dying will lead to new life, new discoveries, new
hope and new vision. And through the dying, God calls, reaching
out to all people, and those who hear the call and respond become
the means by which God continues to call others.

I have told part of the story of my own calling because I am sure
the dynamics of my life mirror the lives of others who are called.
Sometimes we can only see the trace of God's hand with hindsight.
Some things we can't see at all. As to my own future, there are glim-
mers and, increasingly, bright shafts of light, but the way forward is
still one of choice and obedience. My own calling has become
much less an exercise of finding my own chosen path, in a self-cen-
tred sort of way, as of keeping myself free enough always to choose
God, and of trusting enough to follow wherever the wind of the
Spirit blows.

## 9

## Being There

Some time ago, a couple, Brian and Suzette Gibbs, with their three beautiful young daughters, Lucy, Gemma and Alice, came to live in our village. They have since moved away, but I still see them from time to time. The youngest daughter, Alice, is an extraordinary person: bright, open and very loving, in spite of having cerebral palsy which affects her walking and which causes other health problems and pain. A few years ago, when Alice was nine, we sat in her garden sipping lemonade and had a conversation about friends and God.

For me, it was memorable. At that time I was the leader of the family service in our local church, a service which Alice and her family attended. When they would arrive at church, I would usually go and welcome them. Alice always greeted me with open arms. She and her sisters seemed to like the services, and often made comments afterwards which showed they had been paying close attention to what had gone on. I felt that the girls genuinely believed in God and were not coming to church because of social convention. I was especially intrigued about Alice. What sense did she make of God and of a world which was patently unfair? How did she see her disability?

And so, one bright afternoon in June, I found myself sitting with Alice in her flower-filled garden, talking about God. What emerged was a strong, vivid and down-to-earth faith, laced with humour, gentleness and wisdom. I asked her to tell me how she knew God was real. Alice had no hesitation in describing her relationship with God: 'He's there and he's helping you. When you're in trouble you know he's there. If you're worried, feel him, and he'll help. I hear him in my mind, but not by my ears. He's saying "don't worry", and he's hoping that we'll be loving more and not worrying.' After that, she added, 'I think that God needs our help.'

When I asked what type of help God needed from us, Alice spoke of prayer. 'If I could,' she said, 'I would spend my whole life praying,' and Alice told me of praying for fighting in the world to end, and that any accidents that happen wont be 'too bad'. She prays for the safety of beef, and for babies and baby milk. 'I'm not selfish,' she assured me, 'but I do pray a bit for me. I'm not praying for some miraculous cure, but I wish something here would happen to help me.' And then, without a trace of self-pity, she said simply, 'My biggest birthday present ever would be to lose this' – and she pointed at her legs which are badly affected by the cerebral palsy. There was no bitterness, just frustration and longing.

We sat in the hot sun, having this conversation in a matter-of-fact way, and several times I could not speak. Her awareness, her faith, her courage and her familiar comments about God overwhelmed me. I did not know what I had been expecting, but I was not prepared for a faith so simple and so real. She used no religious language, and she seemed to make no division between her understanding of God and the rest of her life. God was one of her friends.

Alice went on to talk about love, and about how much she loved her family. She described her own heart, bursting with love that she could not possibly communicate in words: 'You can't just say to someone "I love you very, very much," because you love them much, much more than that!'

I asked about her best friend, and why she was her best friend. Alice thought for a moment and then answered, 'She is someone who won't race off, someone who will wait for me. She's very fast, but she's slow for me.' I suppose that is one of the most beautiful definitions of friendship I have ever heard: *she's very fast, but she's slow for me.*

Before I left, Alice said something that seemed to sum up the entire human struggle with relating to God, and the need we have of other people. Speaking very calmly and wistfully, she said, 'I know that God's here to talk it all out to, but he's not here the way you're here, and you need someone here.'

Alice is right. We do need someone here, someone who can care for us and show us the love of God just by being here. We need to be here for one another. And we need people like Alice to remind us.

We need to do better at being here for one another. We need to make the leap of the imagination that will allow us to see other people as *real* as we see ourselves. We can't *talk* about things like empathy and compassion: we have to live them. God didn't tell us about how much he loves us, he showed us in Jesus and he still shows us in innumerable ways. At some point we have to take the risk to break through the walls we have constructed, whether they are walls of bigotry or blindness, fear or pride, and reach out to those around us. Jesus was love in action, and he tried to show us that we could not live his love in isolation. We have to live his love with each other. God's love never stops with just one of us, it envelopes us all. Each of us as an individual is unique and infinitely precious – but we're also connected.

Chris Collingwood, a priest and writer, tells the story of once riding on an underground train during rush hour. He recalls looking around at the other passengers, and viewing them dispassionately as detached, separate and anonymous. Then, as he explains,

> quite without warning I was taken out of myself and transported by the experience of a love in which everyone in the compartment, myself included, was held, and which gave to each a real and unique personal identity. No longer were they faceless individuals. Rather at the deepest level of all they were seen to be part of one another, loved, and of infinite value and significance. In my mind's eye I saw each person going home, to be met and welcomed by people to whom he or she mattered. I saw an endless variety of persons in their unique individualities and yet bound together in a fundamental unity from beyond.[1]

That experience had a tremendous effect on Chris, and he expresses a deep gratitude for having been given, even for a moment, 'an awareness of all things and all people grounded in the love of God'.

If Chris's flash of insight was indeed from God, then perhaps it could inspire us to take seriously, as part of our God-given nature, a commitment to the well-being of all that God has made. Such an awareness could inform our discussions about environmental issues, animal welfare, the ethics of scientific research and the issues of human justice I raised earlier in this book.

It is self-evident that we share the planet, the air, the oceans and seas and all the earth's resources, albeit unfairly distributed. It's pretty obvious, also, that we all experience life as physical bodies. 'The hope for our world is for humans to connect, to recognise each other as joined by our common creation and humanity. Apart from whatever it is that we do with our lives, we all exist as bodies, and that is a good place to start to learn to accept our common existence.'[2]

## Reaching out in love

But what if, in addition to seeing each other as bodies sharing a physical connectedness, we could imagine ourselves as part of each other in a different way? What if we really believed that we were all of infinite value, bound together in, and part of, the unity of God's love? What if it was possible to form communities of people who were committed to living in the light of this awareness? Could it be that we might go some way towards creating heaven on earth?

The American theologian William Countryman believes that moving towards 'a world in which the principle of love is taken seriously will be a long and difficult process,' but one that is vital.

> The world will not be safe for any of us until it is safe for all. However difficult the principle of love, and however demanding and hard at times to define, love is the only moral principle that opens a door to the future. When I truly believe that I am as human as you and you are as human as I, that God loves us indistinguishably, I shall begin building a different kind of world.[3]

Jesus once told a story about a man who was mugged. All the people who would have been expected to help the injured man passed by on the other side of the road. It was eventually a despised outsider who cared for the man. After Jesus told this story, he asked his listeners, one of whom was a lawyer, "'Who do you think behaved like a neighbour to the man who had been mugged?" "The one who showed mercy on him", answered the lawyer. Jesus then replied, "Go and do the same"' (Luke 10:29–37).

Go, and in your life reach out to those who are in need. Reach out across the divides of race, sex, gender, age, position, education, faith, wealth, health, lifestyle and all the other factors that make us feel separate and distant from each other. Be prepared to show kindness to those who are not your natural friends and allies. Reach out to those who may or may not be aware of God's mercy, knowing that in doing so you are reaching out to someone beloved of God.

My mother used to collect stray people, the way some people collect stray animals. She never did it on purpose, it's just that she'd meet someone who was sad or lonely, or without a home for a short time, and the next thing I'd know is that Mrs So-and-So would be joining us for supper. After we had stopped living on the boat, we moved into my grandparent's home on Long Island. It was a large house, with two spare bedrooms even when all our family was at home. People who had fallen on hard times, recovering alcoholics, and homeless and jobless foreigners – my mother welcomed them all. For the years I was in secondary school, I can't remember a Thanksgiving dinner without at least a few extra guests, some speaking only broken English and some dabbing their eyes off and on throughout the meal. My mother would let them talk, cry, eat and sleep, and eventually, after a few days or weeks, they would be able to sort out their lives and move on.

At the time, I took all this for granted, as a way that everyone behaved, but now I see how much my mother went beyond what was expected socially or what was convenient for her. She took a risk by inviting some of these people into our home, and she went out on a limb as she helped them to pick up the pieces of their fractured lives. Most of all, she gave them sanctuary: a place to rest and be safe and regain their strength and confidence.

It's not possible to love your neighbour like this unless you know something of God's love for you. Your love for others will reflect how you know yourself to be loved by God, and your view of other people as also beloved of God. Your attitude and behaviour will not be based on any thought of having earned God's love or of being better than anyone else. Doing good to others will not be seen as a worthy project that you have initiated and that you draft God in to support. If it is, it will fail, because at some point you will feel that you should be owed something in return, some sign of gratitude, and the love of God does not reach out in order to get. It reaches out because it has to; it gives because it must.

God loves because God *is* love. God loves because God has to love. God loves because that is the whole point of life, of our existence. There is nothing higher. There is no other virtue or goal or concept that is higher than love. There is nothing that takes precedence over love. There is nothing that outranks love.

Everything must be held up to the light of love, and measured against the principle of love. Whatever it is, if it does not measure up to love, it is not the best and it is not the good news that Jesus came to show and that he lived out in his earthly life.

Without this understanding of the pre-eminence of love, I do not think that it is possible to build the types of communities and societies that I am suggesting, communities where all people are treated with respect, where the weak are given the help they need and the poor are not excluded from events, activities and decision-making. If love is not held to be the highest law there is, then sooner or later something else will creep in and be hailed as the highest good. And because nothing else can be the highest good, it will eventually find itself vying with God.

The clear virtue of justice, if it is placed above love, will become hard-edged and self-serving. The noble principle of freedom, if it is placed above love, will lead to disintegration and a lack of compassion. Any virtue, however high, if placed above love will end up excluding some and diminishing others. Only by exercising the highest virtue of love can we ever build a world that includes and considers all. It is only love that always serves the other, without ignoring the needs and value of the self. It is only love that can hold us all in the complicated, difficult and painful realities we experience, without at some point deciding for one over the other. It is only love that makes true justice and freedom possible.

This, of course is the ideal, an acknowledgement of what God calls us to do. Living it out fully in our lives, and establishing it consistently across the earth, seems hardly possible, but it remains our vision and our goal. We must give love the highest place and serve love as best we can, otherwise we will not be serving God. If God is love, then living in love will be our highest calling.

The late Shelagh Brown and Phil Lawson-Johnston tell the story of a woman called Jo who had been trying to live as a good Christian, but because of having been bullied and humiliated as a child she had lost any sense of self-worth. One day, during a church service, Jo was suddenly overcome with a great feeling of acceptance. She saw vividly how much worth and value she had in Christ, and at that point God became real for her. Jo was able to receive God's love in a new way and let go of all her old hurts and feelings of self-hatred. For the first time, Jo

> really knew that God loved and valued me. From that moment on I didn't only have a new heart. It was strange, but it was as if I had new eyes. I saw everything in a different light. Before I had been so inward looking – and always looking in on myself, and so hurt. But now I had been given new eyes and a new heart, and I was looking out and everything seemed to be so different. I can't explain it. I would look at a field or at flowers, or at the sea or the sky, and there would be some meaning in it all. Everything seemed brighter. And I had a new understanding of people and of God.[4]

Not only was Jo able to feel and accept the love of Christ, but she was able to feel this love for other people, and even see meaning in nature. I wonder whether we are free enough to see that there is meaning in what God has made, and that all of creation is joined by a common inheritance. We must worship only God as God, but we can love trees and stretches of beach and boulders and flowers as parts of creation that are able to convey new insights into the God who is our Source.

John V. Taylor believed that obeying this God requires our openness and response. Sinning comes 'from our refusal of exchange, our shutting off of self so as neither to give nor receive. Being brought to life is the renewal of relationship with this living God and, in him, with all creatures.'[5] If *relationship* is the goal, then sin might also be described as anything that impedes and prevents relationship, initially and primarily with God, but also with other people and the rest of creation. Perhaps our relationships with each other can be whole only to the extent that we are able to open ourselves to and receive the love of God.

## New ways of relating

It is clear that becoming a Christian and following Christ is not intended for us just as isolated individuals, although we can know ourselves loved, saved and accepted as individuals. But we are not to spend our time in competition with each other, each polishing our lives in such a way as to shine as the brightest exhibit in God's showcase. The peace and joy which each of us seeks can only be realised if we are not standing against the possibility of peace and joy for others. As we are being transformed by the renewing of our minds, so we become people who no longer threaten the image of God in others.

Personal freedom becomes the freedom to serve others in the name of Christ, and to be open to be served by others. Personal freedom which is defined by autonomous self-determination is ultimately an illusion, because that type of selfish freedom can only result in bondage to our own self-interest, and all too often the limiting of another's freedom. True freedom must be redefined as submission to Christ and service to others in his name, and will involve, in one of the greatest paradoxes of human existence, a large amount of personal sacrifice.

And yet, we still find it easier to talk about the interrelatedness of the environment than we do about that of communities of people. We still like to think that we can create our own perfect set of friends as we want to, and hang everyone else. Margaret Thatcher famously proclaimed that there was no such thing as society. However, there would be complete anarchy, chaos and social disintegration if there were no society, no sense of belonging in some way to each other, and clearly we do sense a belonging, even though it is fragmented and damaged.

Bill Thatcher, a friend from Seattle, has worked for a long time on issues involved in building genuine community, because of his own need to change how he felt about himself and how he related to other people. Years ago, he became involved with the Foundation for Community Encouragement, a group that helps individuals and organisations to learn how to build and sustain communities characterised primarily by unconditional acceptance. Aspects of this type of acceptance are openness, the willingness to let go of prejudice and blame, the acknowledgement of personal responsibility and the courage and ability to discern how to live more honestly and authentically. Communities based on these principles become places where it is safe to share pain as well as joy, and where people learn to reach out and connect with others in ways which are freeing and enhancing to everyone involved.

This may sound somewhat utopic, but Bill has seen hundreds of lives changed in the many workshops he has led for the Foundation. At first, though, Bill attended a workshop because of the inner turmoil he was experiencing in his personal and spiritual life. Many of the relationships in his life were turning sour, and he was unable to express his thoughts and emotions. He couldn't see any way forward, and he was feeling increasingly isolated and trapped inside himself.

Eventually, Bill realised that the key to his problems lay with how he related to God. He discovered that he was in a battle inside himself over who was God. Was what Bill thought was God really God, or was it just Bill himself? Bill lived with this tension for a while, but he was finally able to admit that he wanted God, with God's priorities and outlook, to be God. But this remains his biggest struggle, and most mornings when he wakes up the first question he asks himself is, 'Who's going to be God today?'

Bill's turning point came when he gave up any presumption that he knew how to be God for himself – then, as he puts it, he 'jumped': if God was responsible for him, he reasoned, then he would 'let God be God'. He became aware that God loved him and that he had value. In common with so many others, Bill describes an experience of feeling alive for the first time.

What had been worrying Bill was that he was afraid that if he surrendered to God, he would not be able to distinguish his own voice from God's. He thought he would be taken over in a way that would nullify his own personality and being, and that he would become even less able to relate to others the way he wanted to. But when he did surrender, he described that what happened was as if God placed his fingers into holes within Bill that ran from the top down, and he felt re-aligned. He also felt a huge sense of relief and liberation – the exact opposite of what he had feared. All of a sudden he was integrated in a new way. For the first time in his life he felt truly free – free from expectations, free from having to get it right. Now when he meets people he asks God what is it that he has to do *to be love* for this person. Everything he does 'passes through God first'.

The way of love also leads to the way of peace, as Henri Nouwen was shown by a severely disabled young man named Adam. Nouwen moved from lecturing in a university to living and helping in a small community for the mentally handicapped and physically disabled. As he cared for Adam, who could neither walk nor speak, Nouwen experienced a new type of peace. This peace was 'rooted in simply being present to each other, a peace that speaks about the first love of God by which we are all held'.[6]

This peace, Nouwen discovered, starts first

> in our own weakness, in those places of our hearts where we feel most broken, most insecure, most in agony, most afraid. Why there? Because there our familiar ways of controlling our world are being stripped away; there we are called to let go from doing much, thinking much, and relying on our self-sufficiency. Right there where we are weakest the peace that is not of this world is hidden.[7]

It is part of the process of letting go and allowing God to show us the peace that he has already given to us, but that we cannot see. When we can trust that 'the God of love has already given the peace we are searching for, we will see this peace breaking through the broken soil of our human condition and we will be able to let it grow fast and even heal the economic and political maladies of our time'.[8]

I remember when Chris and I had not been married long, we had an argument. What it was about I have no idea, but it lasted for several days in a quiet, undertone sort of way. One Sunday afternoon we took a bath together. I brought our disagreement into the bath with us and was arguing my point when I suddenly became aware of Chris sitting behind me, rubbing my back.

All the while I was making my case, his hand was making large circles and stroking my back. The exact details became unimportant, and I stopped talking and let Chris's loving hand calm me. Later, we were able to solve the problem without any fuss, and the whole issue was forgotten. The peace between us was already there, only I was intent on thinking and reasoning it through to a conclusion. When I became quiet and let the peace through, we were both held in that peace and shown the way forward.

I am not suggesting that all the problems between individuals and nations can be solved by being quiet together, or even by taking baths together and massaging each other, though that doesn't sound like too bad a thought! What I am suggesting is that the peace that God wants for us is already ours. If it is real for God, then it can become real for us as we appropriate it in our hearts and minds. We must trust God for the peace, and then live our lives in such a way as to let the peace break through.

When we are living without the peace of God, it is as if we are living in darkness. We can see this darkness in us and in others, just as we can see peace. We see it in ourselves, in our families, our communities and all over our world. It is only God's peace, the peace that we have to accept as something that has already been given to us, that is the light that will dispel the darkness. This peace, this light, is the light of God's love.

There is an old Hasidic story that points to this. One day a rabbi asks his students, 'How can we determine the hour of dawn, when the night ends and the day begins?' One of the students says, 'Is it when you can see the difference between a dog and a sheep?' The rabbi shakes his head. Another student says, 'Is it when you can distinguish between a fig tree and a grapevine?' The rabbi shakes his head again. 'I will tell you,' he says, 'it is when you can look into the faces of other human beings and there is enough light in you to recognise them as your sisters and brothers. Until then, it is night, and the darkness is still with us.'[9]

## 10

# A Mutual Delight

When I was a teenager, I read everything I could to find out about how to be a 'good girl' and how to get relationships 'right'. I hoped that someone somewhere could tell me how to live correctly and how to get rid of everything about myself that seemed to fall beneath the exacting standards of what I imagined was part of living a good Christian life.

However, as I was reading the latest book on *Being Perfect* or whatever it was really called, I realised that the person who had written the book knew nothing at all about what it was like to be me, nor, for that matter, any of my girl friends. He, for it was a he, confidently asserted what young men would be feeling and also what young women would be feeling. He then went on to give his advice about how good Christian young men and women should behave.

I would have heeded his advice if he had shown that he understood – after all, I was aching for good advice – but the more I read, the more obvious it became that he had never spoken openly and honestly to any young women. I read how I would never feel sexual desire until I was married, or, at least, until I was engaged. My fiancé, however, would be having enormous problems controlling his desire for me, but, of course, if he was a true Christian, he would manage. I read how the sight of men's bodies would not turn me on, whereas the sight of women's bodies would bring young men out in hives. I read how my desires were all for love and security, for someone to keep me safe.

I was told authoritatively that I would find the thought of physical contact outside of marriage repulsive. Until my wedding night, I would have had no experience of sex, except for perhaps the infrequent chaste kiss (lips shut, no tongues). The overall message was that women were virtually asexual creatures who only blossomed sexually, and then not too fully, in marriage, while men were doomed to a lifetime of struggling to keep their sexual desires in check. Of course, it was not only possible, it was expected that the only option for Christians was to 'get it right'. Failure in conforming to the sexual ideal was a sign of a disordered personality.

Bottom line, it was the young woman's responsibility to say 'no' to any naughty young man, and it was the young man's responsibility to keep the beast within him under control. It revealed an appalling view of human beings and a debased view of sex.

I can't remember just what it was that finally got to me, but at some point I swore loudly and threw the book as hard as I could across the room, something I don't believe I have ever done to any other book. At that moment I resolved never again to read a Christian book on love and sex – unless it was one that I had written myself!

I kept that vow for a long time, but over the past few years I confess that I have, once again, peeked through the pages of various Christian books on love and sex. Some have been great improvements; some, alas, are still peddling lies. In a way, writing this chapter is an opportunity to fulfil the second part of my promise to myself. Who knows, I may write more on the subject in the future, but this is a chance to look at sexuality in the context of God's love and desire for us.

I have come a long way since I was a teenager in understanding what it means to be human and what it means to be a sexual being, but I have still not found any tidy answers. What I have discovered is a way to look at human desire that is consistent with seeing all that we are as made in the image of God. Our sexual longing, as well as our spiritual longing, is part of our God-given nature. Our sexuality affects more than just the physical: it affects our whole being at many different levels. As such, it can teach us and help us to become who we are meant to be.

Thomas Moore, the writer, theologian and ex-monk, sees our sexual longing as part of the process by which we discover who we are. He believes that the

> intimacy in sex, while always attached to the body, is
> never only physical. Sex always evokes pieces of stories

and fragments of characters, and so the desire and willingness to be sexually transparent is truly an exposure of
the soul. In sex we may discover who we are in ways otherwise unavailable to us, and at the same time we allow
our partner to see and know that individual. As we unveil
our bodies, we also disclose our persons.[1]

Perhaps when we learn to integrate our sexuality with the rest of our
being, we will be able to overcome much of the devastating sense of
alienation that affects so many people in our culture. When we learn
to have honest, creative and integrated sexuality, we will know ourselves in new ways, and out of our own self-acceptance and peace,
we will be able to be more open to others, as human to human, with
all that that entails. We may be able to see our sexuality as a gift, not
only *from* God but, in a sense, as a gift *of* God. Our right-related
sexuality may be one of the most positive and liberating manifesta-
tions of God's life in us. But it is not a straightforward process.

Thomas Moore would have us let go of any hopes to pin sex
down, to define it too tightly. He cautions:

As long as we think of sex in a limited way, as a biological function or even as only a means of communication
or intimacy, we will be mystified by its unexpected turns.
It would be better to recognise from the beginning that
sex is a profound, far-reaching aspect of the soul, bringing together body, emotion and imagination in an intense
experience that can touch every branch of feeling and
meaning, yet one we may never fully understand. It is by
nature mysterious.[2]

I think Moore is right: sex eludes full and precise definition. To
analyse sex from a biological point of view is to miss a great amount
of what sex is all about. To look at reproductive, psychological or
even pathological aspects of sex is not to look at sex as most of us
experience it. It is part of who we are, and yet it is a particularly
complex, mysterious part.

As Elaine Storkey reminds us,

only one aspect of our sexuality is expressed in sexual
intercourse. We also express it in warmth and touch, in
closeness and care for the other persons who are dear to

us. If in our lives there is no sexual union with another, perhaps because we have accepted celibacy, or gone through bereavement, illness or divorce, we are no less fully human and fully sexual. Deeply satisfying human intimacy, whether in marriage or outside, is in the end not dependent on copulation but on a faithful sharing of our hearts and lives with those whom we love, and a longing for their well-being and peace.[3]

## Confusion over sexuality

Our society sends out very mixed messages about sex. Churches also send out mixed messages about it, and most individuals are caught up in a confusing struggle to understand what they feel about their own sexuality, and then what to do about it. We pretend that sex is no longer taboo in our society, but try to discuss it in many situations, and the shutters come down. Oh, we laugh about it, snigger, mock, ogle and gawp, but we do not seem to be able to talk about it lovingly and gently. We can accept that some people need sex therapy, or that others need psychotherapy for sexual problems, but to talk about sex in a measured but light, spiritual but down-to-earth way doesn't seem to happen that often.

I can let you know if I am feeling physically hungry, or if I am feeling in need of friendship, or if I am feeling spiritually hungry, but I cannot tell you that I am feeling sexually in need. It is not typically acceptable in many arenas in our society to hint at sexual desire, legitimate or otherwise. There are, of course, exceptions: at weddings it is acceptable to tease the couple about the wedding night, and in situations where sex is for sale the one who is paying can ask for what they want. But weddings are only occasional events, and purchasing sex is hardly a Christian ideal. It is among my close women friends that I have best been able to discuss sex in an open and helpful way, and I am grateful for many such conversations over the years – aids to sanity and self-acceptance!

I am not suggesting that we must all suddenly start talking about sex, but I think it is important that we recognise the odd *demimonde* to which we have relegated it in our society. I think that our discomfort and confusion about sex tells us something about its power. We have a strong reluctance to give it the space in our lives that it requires, except as a joke or as something lewd.

How many of us can remember first being told about sex? Was it by a loving parent or parents? Was it by a friend or a teacher? Did you feel able to ask your parents any or all of the questions you had about sex? Did your attempts to talk about sex leave you with positive and joyful feelings, or did you learn to hide what you were really feeling and bury it deep in an area of your being labelled 'Danger' 'Dirty' or 'Keep Out'?

When you think about your sexuality now, do you feel loving and happy, or bitter and sad? Whether or not you ever express your sexuality with another person, do you feel comfortable with who you are, or could you weep with the pain of it all?

One of the lies being told about sex in our society is that everyone is at it. Yet recent research shows that sex is being edged out of many people's lives by the pressure and pace of work, or by having children, which I find particularly ironic, seeing that the arrival of children usually means that sex has taken place. Of course, in the instances of fostering and adoption, this may not necessarily be true for the adopting couple, but it is largely the case for most children in most families. Is having children, therefore, a sure way of killing sex? Was the sex really 'alive' in the first place?

Another lie about sex is that, if you're in a good relationship, preferably marriage, sex will be easy and wonderful. Or that if you follow certain techniques, all will be well. But sex isn't like that. We humans aren't like that. The whole area of sex is the most subtle, most nuanced, will-o'-the-wisp, contrary, maddening, surprising, frightening, exhilarating area of our beings.

I find it extraordinary that Christians are earnestly diligent about reading improving books on spirituality, going on the occasional retreat and attending worthy conferences, and yet we treat our sexuality in a way we wouldn't treat an unwelcome stray cat. We sweep all our sexual hurt and anger, longing and unfulfilled desire under the carpet, and then we wonder why we're so messed up. Could it be that we need a new approach to even *thinking* about sexuality – never mind *doing* anything about it?

### Accepting our sexuality
I am aware that the title of this chapter is 'A Mutual Delight' and for the rest of it I will offer some positive thoughts about our sexuality and include some writings that help me to think creatively

and joyfully about the relationship between sexuality and God. There may be no easy answers or failsafe solutions to our problems with sex, but I believe that if God created us as sexual beings, and we are made in God's image, then we ought to be able to find more true delight in our sexuality than perhaps many of us have done so far.

Instead of using our sexuality as a gift that can help to heal and make whole and give value, too often, it seems, our sexual relationships implode and leave us feeling more isolated and cut off from other people. Our sexuality feels as if it is more acutely vulnerable to the distortions of sin than other aspects of our natures. It seems much easier to sort out a misunderstanding between friends or business colleagues, but when something goes wrong between two lovers, the pain and effort it takes to get the relationship back on course seems much greater. I wish we had been given more of an insight into how Jesus was able, as fully human and fully divine, to live as a sexual being without sinning. We may wish to see our sexuality as a part of sharing and enriching love, but how do we do it? All too often, our sexuality is a source of shame, alienation, confusion and emotional pain.

Just as I know that complete sexual licence is not the answer, so also I know that repression and becoming closed in on oneself is not the answer either. Becoming open and healthy with our sexuality takes a constant vigilance against using sex as a substitute for genuine intimacy, and also against shutting ourselves off from other people in all but the narrowest of ways that excludes any possibility of sexual desire and arousal. It seems, in short, that it is easier to get sex wrong than it is to get it right, even though I sometimes wonder whether it would not be such a struggle if many of those in power in the churches had not had such a debased view of sex and our bodies, especially female bodies, at certain times in the history of Christianity. Even some of the great theologians, partly because of their culture and partly because of their limited and skewed understanding of human reproduction, railed against sexual desire and the temptations to sexual sin. It did not help when otherwise reasonable and intelligent men like Tertullian, writing in the late first and early part of the second century, called women 'the gateway to the devil', or when, in the tenth century, the pious Odo of Cluny considered that 'to embrace a woman is to embrace a sack of manure'. Sex, almost more than any other area of human activity, is one which the Church has tried to control.

In order to love well, we must give of ourselves, but just what does that mean? What it must not mean is a giving of the self in such a way that the self is lost. We must not allow ourselves to be turned, or turn other people, into objects that can be discarded when no longer fancied. That is damaging, not liberating and healing. To love with self-giving love means to move away from concentration on the self towards the focus on the other. It also means to be open and generous with one's own self so that the other can enter into one's true self. It is about vulnerability as well as about making space for another, space for the other to bring their thoughts and feelings and find a place where they are respected and safe. The more one loves another with this type of love, the more one is able to discover wholeness and completeness. So, in a paradoxical way, self-giving love actually results in finding and gaining oneself, through love.

But it is a difficult business, remaining open, seeking the good of the other person, inviting closeness, and then being tender and patient with all that the other brings. It is sacrificial in terms of energy and time, and nothing can ever be promised at the start of, or at any other stage in, such a journey. That is why, along with the heightened sense of awareness and twinges of well-being, sexual love, even between long-term partners, can be a frightening prospect. What will be demanded of me and how will the other react? Will they be gentle and fair with me and my desires? There is always only ever one way to find out, and that is by taking the first step.

At times I have been tempted, but I am committed to resisting the temptation, to offer specific advice about specific situations. Of course there are different things to be said about what is appropriate for single people, engaged and married couples, and those divorced or widowed. Of course there are distinctions to be made for the wide variety of relationships we experience, but in this chapter I intend to suggest principles that relate to our sexuality overall. Although details are not included, I have come to believe that the new commandment Jesus gave to his followers is the key advice for all our relationships. 'A new commandment I give to you, that you love one another; even as I have loved you, that you also love one another' (John13:34). Elsewhere, his command is twofold: love God with all your heart and soul and mind, and love your neighbour as yourself (Matthew 22:37–40 and Luke 10:27). If our sexuality is truly part of who we are, then we must include it in our thinking in how to live out the law of love, and not relegate it to a separate compartment.

Working out how to interpret love of God and neighbour is the answer to how to conduct relationships. Although we will never be perfect while we live on earth, we can become more and more aware of who God is, and how God's love is best served and lived. What does it take? Among other things, an astonishing amount of honesty, self-knowledge and the desire to love and obey God.

Honesty and self-knowledge need to go hand in hand: without self-knowledge it is easy to slip up, often in the same way, again and again. Without honesty, we can fool ourselves into ascribing more worthy motives for what we do. Self-knowledge means that I can't just 'find' myself in certain situations; I will know what I am getting myself into. Honesty means that I will think through the likely consequences of all that I do. My love for God will cause me to want to obey what I understand to be his will. There will always be risks and the potential for either deceiving ourselves, misjudging ourselves, or of not loving God enough. But I believe that is far better a way to go through life than trying to match a pre-ordained set of rules against every conceivable situation.

So often it is not just the elements in any given situation, but the personalities and conditions of the people involved. What might be fun and freeing and legitimate for me to do with one friend, might be deeply unwise for me to do with another. When I was a student at university, I had a friend, an older male student, who loved giving me massages. We were perfectly at ease with each other, we both wanted to stay 'just friends' and our times together, though delightfully sensual, never became sexual. I had other male friends who, if they had offered to give me a massage, I would have had to decline, either because I didn't trust myself or them. I knew that our relationships would have escalated sexually, and I didn't want them to.

The highest law for me to follow is the law of love. The law of love also demands that I will never coerce or force another against their will. This way, life can still have the spontaneity I have praised so highly earlier in the book. I will not close myself to experiences on the off-chance that they will somehow go wrong, but I will also be attuned to what the Spirit is telling me. It is up to us as honest, mature, self-knowing and God-loving individuals to weigh up each situation. No one else can do it for you, and if you let them, you will be abrogating your free will, your personal responsibility and your position as a unique and beloved child of God.

The younger a person is, the more external guidance and rules they need. But as people grow into mature adulthood, the guidance should be able to come more from within. We are spiritually accountable as members of the Body of Christ, but the primary line of accountability for the mature person and their sexual behaviour is his or her own relationship with God.

I know very mature Christians who belong to a small group of friends who support and pray for one another, and when necessary act as confessors. I have had the privilege and responsibility of always having at least one, if not more, good Christian friends to whom I can go with anything that is on my heart or my mind. For several years I have also had an accepting and wise spiritual advisor.

## Sexuality and spirituality

God's love for us is so strong and so committed that it has been compared to the passion that human lovers feel for each other. In the Old Testament particularly, God is often described as being jealous about his special people, the Israelites, when they went after false gods. God is shown as being hurt or angry over what his people have done, as well as filled with delight when they have responded to his love.

The Song of Solomon in the Bible is an incredibly rich dialogue poem between two lovers. It is also explicitly sensual and sexual. Some scholars suggest that it can be read as a symbolic poem about God's love for his people, and that may be so, but for me the beautiful and graphic dialogue between the two lovers, the young Solomon and the Shulammite maiden, makes any further symbolism difficult and unnecessary. However, on whatever level one reads it, it is clearly filled with passionate images and overtly sexual allusions:

I slept, but my heart was awake.
Hark! My beloved is knocking.
'Open to me, my sister, my love,
my dove, my perfect one;
for my head is wet with dew,
my locks with the drops of the night.'

I had put off my garment, how could I put it on?
I had bathed my feet, how could I soil them?
My beloved put his hand to the latch,
and my heart was thrilled within me.
I arose to open to my beloved,
and my hands dripped with myrrh,
my fingers with liquid myrrh,
upon the handles of the bolt.
(Song of Solomon 5:2–5)

Ancient mystics and contemplatives recorded moments of emotion for God that we would recognise as erotic. Saint Teresa had visions in which Jesus would be repeatedly plunging a burning arrow into her heart, and there are many paintings and statues, some recent and some hundreds of years old, that reveal a bringing together of the spiritual and the sensual. The two often overlap, and are connected in many people's minds and experiences. I know more than one person who has found times of prayer and spiritual intensity to be times also of increased sensual awareness.

Carter Heyward, an Episcopalian priest and professor at Harvard, Massachusetts, bases much of her theology on the assumption that our sexuality is both made and blessed by God, and when used aright ushers us into the realm of the divine.

She explains:

To speak of the erotic or of God is to speak of power in right relation . . . Real lovemaking is not simply genital manipulation . . . lovemaking is a form of justicemaking . . . As a western Christian, I am interested in helping to lay to rest the pernicious dualisms between sex and God, sexuality and spirituality, body and spirit, and pleasure and goodness, which historically the church has used to dull the edges of human and divine experience. By lit-

erally splitting us in two, the dominant ideology of western culture has rendered us – to the extent we are white
male-identified – flattened facsimiles of fully human
beings. We have been stripped – spiritually, physically,
emotionally, and intellectually – of our capacities to
delight in ourselves, one another, the creation, and its
holy wellsprings.[4]

Heyward goes on to develop a theology that many Christians
would consider sexually liberal. Although I don't share all her con-
clusions, I am challenged and invigorated by her honesty and
integrity, and I agree with much of what she sees as wrong with the
Church and western society.

For Heyward, the erotic is a positive power, and by being in
touch with our senses, as well as our feeling and intelligence, we can
come to know God. She writes that 'the erotic is known most
immediately through our senses. We see, hear, touch, smell, and taste
the divine, who is embodied between and among us insofar as we
are moving more fully into, or toward, mutually empowering relationships in which all creatures are accorded profound respect and
dignity.'[5] That may sound somewhat sweeping, but her point is that
erotic longing is a longing for wholeness, for experiencing oneness
with God, and with other people. When we deny our longing, we
deny ourselves the possibility of reaching out to others and discovering them, and ourselves, more fully.

If we continually refuse to include our sexual awareness in the
rest of our lives of faith, not only will we diminish our understanding of God, but we will also be keeping artificial and unhelp-
ful divisions between us and other people. Being sexually aware is
not the same as being sexually active; rather, it involves bringing
our whole selves into the light of God's healing and transforming
love, and allowing ourselves to connect with others.

Heyward also writes about the de-humanising effects of a per-
verted eroticism such as sadomasochism, and sees our only hope of
healing as the liberating power and love of God. She would urge us
to learn how to share power in our relationships, so that we can
avoid exploitation and fear and create relationships of safety and
tenderness.

One of our deepest yearnings is for mutuality:

We have seen it through a glass dimly. We know it is here among us, and not here; now, but not yet. We live in these tensions of affirmation and lamentation. What we want most terrifies us most – passionate connectedness with one another that will draw us sharply into our identities as persons in relation in our work and in our love.[6]

## Identity and belonging

Not only did God make sex necessary for the continuation of the human race, he also made it a truly mystical way to heal and be healed, to know and be known, to reach out and to be held. Physical love touches more than our bodies: it touches our souls and spirits too. In our world of loneliness and alienation, with so many of us not really knowing who we are and whether or not anyone really loves us, sex in its fitting place can heal us and make us whole. It can help to reveal to us who we are, as I once tried to express in a poem:

> Your love has given me a shape,
> given me a name:
> Wonderful, Lovely-to-be-loved,
> Fire, Mermaid, Peace.
> You are Beautiful, Wild Waves,
> Lightening Storm, Gentleness, Wisdom.
> It is as you stroke the curves of my body
> that I learn my shape.
> It is as you speak to me
> that I learn my name.

Accepting love helps us to know who we are. It is only by relating to others that I can learn who I am. Through the special touch of a lover, I am able to learn things about myself that I could not learn in any other way.

There is in sexual longing a large amount of spiritual longing, and vice versa. When I was about eighteen I wrote a poem that, even as I wrote it, I was not sure whether it was primarily about physical love or spiritual longing. Somehow, it was about both. It began:

> I was christened by the heat of the fire,
> By the hard hearth stones I grew

> In light and warmth enough for everyone
> But only I saw and came,
> Only I felt and came.

And after tracing my longing and searching for an elusive, mysterious Something, the poem ended:

> Many nights when sad hands
> Felt only locks of cold brass,
> Doorknobs pinched in whitened wood,
> Until one night to find it –
> To be drawn to the fresh smiling
> Calm burning. Always lit.
> I was christened by the heat of the fire
> By the hard hearth stones I knelt
> Every night to kneel and melt
> Making in the molding darkness
> Different shadows on the wall.

Some years later, I reworked the poem for a cycle of love poems that were set to music by the composer Richard Lambert. I changed the last verse to:

> I am christened by the heat of your fire,
> Every night we kneel and melt,
> Making in the molding darkness
> Different shadows on the walls.

No more ambiguity between the physical and spiritual! I came down firmly on the side of sexuality, for the sake of the song cycle. But when I read my original version, I am still unable to disregard my sense that I was writing just as much about my longing and searching for Christ, as I was writing about my search for an imaginary human lover. Our sexuality and sensuality are part of our spiritual awareness, and there can, at times, be a cross-over between spiritual and sexual longing, as many writers and artists have expressed throughout the centuries. When I was at university I used to write psalms, as well as poems. This is one that survived:

> I have felt the hands of an angel
> And the flood of your power.
> I know the rhythm of your love

And the wash of your peace.
Lord, take us into your soft valleys,
Lead us into your fields,
Set us loose in the starlight of your dance.
Then let us praise your name with our bodies –
Swinging round and round
In the garden of your word.

Whether or not it 'works' as a psalm for anyone else but me, I have no idea, but reading it now I am struck by the sensual imagery.

Thinking back, at about the same time I had the bizarre experience of having some of my poems rejected by the college magazine on the grounds that they were too 'pornographic'. I remember my outrage! They were not remotely pornographic, but only rather sensual. I think this type of confusion carries on today, with people shying away unnecessarily from legitimate sensuality.

In another poem I tried to capture the experience of having met someone for the first time, and yet feeling as if we had known each other for ever. I described being introduced to each other, and ended it in this way:

And there we stood,
bared to the soul,
an ancient recognition
whose dawn began before our time.
We have come to where we should:
the tangled maze has led to good.

There is in some meetings with other people the sense of belonging, of coming home, of having found a place where we are safe, where we can risk being vulnerable. These are feelings that many people have had about God, and they are, at heart, a mystery, impossible to analyse fully in an objective sense. I suppose that's why I have resorted to poetry when trying to write about sex and God and love. Coming closer to God brings one closer to a place where we can know and be known, both by God and by other people, and yet not be afraid.

There is something about God's love, love that is always reaching out, always offering itself, that, if we let it, can get through all our masks and barriers, and touch us in the core of our beings. We can know this love in times of prayer, in worship, in creativity and in nature, or at any other time we are able to lift the veil and let God in.

A further miracle is that God allows this love to be shared between people, and offers it to us if we are willing to let go of our insistence on perfection and our drive always to get it 'right'. For love will always be a mystery, it will always elude precise definition and description. It will come when we are least expecting it, and it will rarely, if ever, appear on demand. What we must do is to live our lives in such a way that we remain open to the God of love. We can cultivate an open heart and a receptive spirit, and learn to look for opportunities to give love, as well as to receive it.

We can learn to love ourselves and accept the bodies we have been given. We can accept physical love, and see it as one of the ways God has provided for our delight and our healing. We can take care to build relationships in which mutual trust and respect and honesty can flourish. We can pledge never to violate another, and never to seek to diminish their sense of self-worth. We can learn to be selfless, without ever giving away our integrity.

Hopefully, we can also learn to take risks and to take ourselves more lightly. We can acknowledge and listen to our longings for closeness, and be glad that it is possible for us to know and be known. Above all, and no matter what, in the middle of our raggedness and need, our longing and ache, we can entrust ourselves to the One who is our Desire beyond all other desires, in whose love we are always held and in whose embrace we can come to remember who we are.

## The Valley of Shadows

Once when I was in an English class in secondary school, we were given the rather odd assignment of writing our own obituaries. We had to write them in the third person, as if for a newspaper, and say the things we would like to have written about us when we die. We were free to choose at what age and why we had 'died'. I wrote about myself having died when I was very old, after a lifetime of good works and impressive creativity. I recounted some of my loving gestures and actions, my hidden kindnesses, my selfless service. I catalogued my impressive accomplishments in a variety of fields and remarked on the likely lasting effects of my love, wisdom and work. By the end of the exercise I was nearly in tears, grieving for the elderly, wonderful me that had just passed away!

It may have been just a class assignment, but I have not forgotten it and from time to time I catch myself playing an occasional game of obituaries. It isn't morbid, and sometimes it helps me to remember what's really important in life.

A more pithy exercise is playing the delightful game of 'gravestone'. I doubt I'm the only one who's ever tried to compose the perfect phrase for summing up my entire life. I'm sure I'm not the only one who's searched for those few choice words that capture the essence of who I am. I started this game when we lived in a little Tudor cottage that backed on to the village churchyard. Our garden was separated from the churchyard by a tall brick wall, but the view from our first-floor window was of all the gravestones, old and new, and I was faced with these reminders of death every day for nearly ten years. Playing gravestones became a fairly good indicator of how I was feeling about myself. On some days I would come up with phrases such as 'she was loved' or 'she loved well' or even the comfortable cliché, 'greatly missed', but there were other days when I'd decide that 'she was a tosser' probably summed me up rather better!

Death. It's ugly, obscene, capricious, callous, pig-headed and downright outrageous. It has no sense of timing, no manners and no heart. Why don't all the nasty, cruel, evil people die, very young, and leave this world to those who are trying to spread a little happiness along the way? When I was in school one friend died on his motorcycle when he was driving, high on drugs. Another friend jumped out of a window when he was severely depressed as a result of abusing drugs. Yet another friend had a heart attack at the age of thirty-one, after years of living in the fast lane. Tragic as these deaths were, there was at least an obvious cause and effect, but what about the people who were just in the wrong place at the wrong time, or who caught a fatal disease? How could the kind, clean-living, positive-thinking, much-loved, everything-to-live-for Linda McCartney die of *cancer*? It's just NOT FAIR!

It is hard for us to come to terms with death, whether we are contemplating our own death or the death of someone we love. But, in the words of the old truism, death is a fact of life. Apart from being born, death is the only other absolutely certain event of our lives. In one sense, we start to die, physically, from the moment we are born. Giving a baby life is, at the same time, giving them the assurance of death.

Life as we know it, death and life after death are all part of God's reality. God inhabits eternity, but, because of Jesus, God also entered our time- and death-limited existence. God has experienced our life on earth, physical death and a new life after death. We can trust, even though we may not understand, that the thread of our existence is unbroken, even after we die.

Still, death is hard. When my father died, I immediately felt that my own life was over. Emotionally, I just stopped. I couldn't think about the future or any plans I had. The routines of life seemed pointless, and for several months I just went through the motions of survival. I could hardly make the effort to smile. In fact, smiling seemed like a betrayal of my love for my father, and so I existed through those first few months in something of a daze, with a long face and an aching heart. Everything inside me hurt.

Of course, it was infinitely worse for my mother. After all, she had been married to my father for over forty-four years. Her shock and gloom lasted for several years. Observing her, and myself, I learned how confusing and exhausting grief could be. I remember when I flew back to America for the funeral, the customs man in the US airport asked whether the purpose of my trip was business or pleasure. I realised that, as far as customs was concerned, I was not on business, but I could not bring myself to answer 'pleasure'. All I could think to say was, 'I am here to bury my father.' Thankfully, he looked at me kindly, said 'Bless you, ma'am', and waved me through with no further questions. I felt so weary I could hardly move.

I remember being particularly struck by a past episode of *Silent Witness*, the television programme based around the work of a pathologist. This episode dealt with a helicopter crash, and the sudden death of 14 men. We, the audience, were shown the bodies, ready for autopsy, ashen grey, limp and drained of life. We saw the grieving wives and distraught colleagues. We watched the lead character of the show, Dr Sam Ryan, as she studied the bodies intently, looking for clues to explain exactly how the men died.

At another point in the programme, we heard her lecturing budding pathology students preparing for their first post-mortems. She told them that they would soon be handling what was once a living, breathing person, loved and now missed, who had once had all the dreams and hopes that they, the living, still had. It was a very heavy programme, and stirred up lots of feelings about death.

It made me think of how I had seen my father's body in the funeral parlour, before the lid of his coffin was closed. Years earlier, I had also seen his father and his uncle in their open coffins. I thought about how their skin looked, and how I was certain that, whoever they had been, and whoever they now were, they no longer resided in their bodies.

The morning after that particular episode of *Silent Witness*, I discovered one of my peahens had died. A few days before, she had seemed a bit unwell, and so I had put her into a pen in our barn. Here she was, less than a week later, quite dead. I took her body to the vet and asked for a post-mortem, because I wanted to know what had killed her and whether the rest of my peafowl, and possibly my chickens, were at risk. The vet found that she had had a parasite that could affect my other peafowl, and I was advised to treat them with medication. In the end, I only managed to catch the one other peahen, and with some difficulty squirted the required dose down her throat. It must have worked, because she is still alive. In fact, shortly after that, she laid two eggs. Happily, all the males survived even without medication.

That same day, one of my cats became so ill that I had to take her to the vet. I was told she was probably dying of a kidney infection. I felt surrounded by death. The memory of the images of the corpses I had seen the night before on television, along with finding my dead bird, and then having to nurse an ailing cat, made me very aware of the inevitability of death. Death may be natural and universal, I thought, but why does it seem so often to come like a cruel surprise or a dark, obscene prank? Why can't we just skip death and get on with the more spiritual existence of eternal life? Why, if I believe in an afterlife, can't I take death more lightly?

We've probably seen or heard of places in the world where people have a much more pragmatic attitude towards death. The dead are still mourned, but in a much more up-front manner than we do in our western culture. I remember once meeting a group of wailing women on a remote road in Greece. I could hear them long before I could see them, coming around a corner on a narrow winding mountain road. They were dressed in black from head to toe, and with tears streaming down their faces they would fling their arms out and then beat their chests. Theirs were the universal gestures of the inconsolable.

We were told by a man walking with us that a relative had died and that the women were expected to weep and wail. After the public display, the formal time of grieving would be over. Of course, for the deceased person's closest family and friends, the grieving would carry on in private, but the loud crying and dramatic gestures were the socially acceptable way of dealing with death.

Not so in England and other places in the western world. We try to keep a stiff upper lip, and feel terribly embarrassed if we break down during an otherwise dignified funeral service. We're allowed to send cards and flowers, give a few extra hugs and meaningful squeezes, but definitely no weeping and wailing – at least not in public.

In some of the southern states of America, there is a very different approach to death. Some Afro-Caribbean Americans say goodbye to their loved ones with a jazz procession through the streets. The procession begins with mournful hymns which eventually turn into exultant jazz. The heavy atmosphere of the funeral is replaced by the energy of a carnival.

Tony Campolo once told the story of a funeral he went to in New York. Tragically, a well-liked teenager had died. The pastor addressed his sermon to the young man's body, placed in an open casket at the front of the church. He listed all the good things that he could remember the young man had done, and added tributes that other people had told him.

After a lengthy time praising the deceased, the pastor walked over to the casket, slammed down the lid, and said in a loud voice, 'Goodbye and Good night!' And then, with the most dramatic timing, he went on to say how the young man could be sure of waking up to a 'Good morning' in heaven that would never end. The service of mourning became a time of celebration in honour of the God of resurrection and eternal life. As Tony Campolo said, it was a funeral he would never forget, a funeral that managed, with incredible style, to focus first on the person who had died and then onto the One who promises life after death.

But what exactly does Christianity teach about death? It seems there are two main ways of looking at death: one is as a natural consequence of our earthly existence, and the other is as a type of curse, part of the result of sin. As Paul put it, 'the sting of death is sin, and the power of sin is the law. But thanks be to God who gives us the victory through our Lord Jesus Christ' (1 Corinthians 15:56–57). If human beings had never sinned, the implication is that there would be no death. But it is not as if death is some sort of punishment; rather, it is the inevitable consequences of our having free will and life on earth.

It is Jesus who holds the key to our understanding of death. When he died and was brought back to life, he destroyed the power of death once and for all. Even though human beings still die, if we are followers of Christ we have been promised eternal life.

Towards the end of his time on earth, Jesus tries to explain to his disciples that he is going away. He does not want his friends to be frightened or worried. He says to them:

> 'Do not be worried and upset. Believe in God and believe also in me. There are many rooms in my Father's house, and I am going to prepare a place for you. I would not tell you this if it were not so. And after I go and prepare a place for you, I will come and take you to myself, so that you will be where I am. You know the way that leads to the place where I am going.' (John 14:1–4)

Straight away, Thomas replies, 'No we don't. We haven't any idea where you are going, so how can we know the way?' Jesus then says to him, 'I am the way and the truth and the life.'

Whatever life after this life will be, it will be a place where Jesus is. Jesus makes it sound like a place of familiarity and fellowship. Wherever it is, it will not be a void in endless space, but a place where people can 'live'. It will feel like home.

Elsewhere in the New Testament, Paul goes on one of his flights of logic, reasoning that because Jesus has been raised from the dead, we too have eternal life. The curse of death has been broken in spiritual terms:

> Death came into the world because of what one man [Adam] did, and it is now because of what this other man [Christ] has done that now there is the resurrection from the dead . . . Every human being has a body just like Adam's, made of dust, but all who become Christ's will have the same kind of body as his – a body from heaven. Just as each of us now has a body like Adam's, so we shall some day have a body like Christ's. (1 Corinthians 15:21, 47–49)

What Paul is describing is a supernatural, spiritual body, one that is fit for living for ever, outside our limited dimensions of space and time. After his resurrection, Jesus could appear at will, walking along a road or standing inside a room. He ate and drank, but he was most decidedly different. It was as if his body could do what his mind or spirit wanted it to, rather than have his actions determined more by the laws of gravity, time and space. Sometimes his friends did not recognise him, and it was only in his actions that they knew for sure it was Jesus.

The last book of the Bible, Revelation, is filled with extraordinary imagery about a new heaven and a new earth. Revelation was written by the apostle John, when he was an old man, imprisoned on the Greek island of Patmos. Some might say perhaps he had a little too much sun and retsina, but his vision is a magnificent, strange, complicated and mysterious picture of what life will be like when there is no more sin, suffering and death.

He describes a beautiful heavenly city, and then adds:

> There shall be nothing in the city which is evil; for the throne of God and of the Lamb will be there, and His servants will worship him. And they shall see his face; and his name shall be written on their foreheads. And there will be no night there no need for lamps or sun – for the Lord God will be their light; and they shall reign for ever and ever. (Revelation 22:3–5)

The vision paints a picture of a world filled with light and beauty, shining with splendour, with everyone happy to acknowledge Jesus as Lord. It is a picture of completion, deep joyful contentment, but still filled with excitement. There is no hint of the boring prospect of sitting around on little puffy clouds all day, strumming harps and complimenting each other on the brightness of our halos! The heaven John sees is an explosion of colour, sound, smell, brilliance and light. He is describing what might be described as a peak experience, but, instead of lasting only a short time, it lasts for ever. I like trying to think about that.

The significant thing about John's heaven is that at the heart of his vision is a loving God. The God in his vision of the future is consistent with the Jesus he knew and loved on earth. The beloved friend who turned his life upside down is the One whom John now sees shining and gleaming with pure light, acknowledged by all to be the Lord.

My aunt, Jan Payne, who was such a huge influence on me when I was growing up, died recently after a long life of living close to God. The day before she died she seemed to be inhabiting two worlds – this one and heaven. Some good friends had come to see her, to say goodbye and to help keep her as comfortable as possible.

Jan lay for most of the time with her eyes shut, but every so often she would speak. One friend started to write down what Jan said.

Jan tried to describe how she was moving in and out of another dimension, where everything was visual – clean, beautiful, white, almost ethereal. Over and over again she would say, 'I wish I could express how much the Lord loves us.' At times she would cry out in praise to God.

Towards the end when she stopped speaking, she said, 'Our God is way beyond what anyone can ask or think or imagine . . . the beauty of the Lord, I just can't believe it! . . . Oh my, I can't take it all in. It's overwhelming. Blessed be the name of the Lord!' Almost the last words she said were, 'Holy, holy, holy, allelulia! The Lord loves us so much.' Her robust and joyous faith during her life had brought her to the doorstep of heaven, and as she started to enter her new life she was not frightened or discouraged; rather, she was full of joy and overwhelmed with the love of God for us.

I think this is the key to thinking about death. No, we don't know what it will be like, even though many people have described near-death experiences that should give us confidence. No, we don't know what it will feel like to carry on living when our bodies have died. But if we can hold fast to our relationship with Jesus, then we can trust that we will continue to exist, and continue to be loved. We can hope to be caught up in a new way in the internal dynamic of the God who exists in relationship; the never-ending dance of the Father, Son and Holy Spirit. We will discover life in a new dimension, we will see with new eyes and hear with new ears, and the colours and sounds will be more beautiful than any we can possibly imagine. C. S. Lewis used to describe our present life as if it was a shadow existence. Only in the life to come will we be exposed to the brilliance of a greater Reality.

Shortly before Jesus was arrested and crucified, he prayed an extraordinary prayer to his heavenly Father. In it, he prays for his disciples, for their protection, unity and joy. Jesus also prays that those in the future who come to believe in him through the faithfulness of his disciples 'may all be one'. Not only does Jesus pray for his followers to be one, but he also asks that 'they may be one as we are one, I in them and you in me, that they may be completely one, so that the world may know that you have sent me and have loved them even as you have loved me' (John 17:22–23).

Our eventual complete oneness with Christ can begin now on earth. The nature of the unity can survive time and space – and death. If we are in Christ, we have already begun to live for ever. In this way, death has 'lost its sting' and we can know that, in the same way we are held close to God now, we will continue to be held close, even after death. We have to go through a change, but we come out on the other side, more, not less, alive. Death, then, is a transition from one way of being alive to another, even better way of being alive.

However, I've got a problem. I can't really think of an existence better than this one. Of course, I can imagine a world in which there is no more disease, no more poverty, no more pain and loss. But what I am really imagining is an improved earth, not a different heaven. So my idea of heaven is just like what we have now, without the pain, without death.

My heaven, wherever it is, will have endless sandy beaches and oceans full of beautiful fish, none of which will want to eat me. Perfect fruit of all varieties will grow all year round, and never be ruined by wasps or weevils. There will be champagne, with no hangovers and no addiction. There will be love-making with no shame or shyness, and no being left wanting more, or other. There will be no misunderstandings, no rejection, no manipulation, no separation. Joy will be pure and deep and never-ending. There will be complete, and not precarious, peace; lasting peace with true justice. No one will ever wish they were someone else, somewhere else. There will be no more wistful thinking, no more ache in the pit of the stomach. No more crying, except for joy and beauty. No more wrenching nostalgia for times, places and people that once were, but are no longer. No more jealousy, envy, misery, despair, anger, alienation. No more pain of any sort. No more injustice, deception, cruelty, betrayal, temptation, downfall, oblivion. Only every living thing saying *yes* to all that God is, for all time – only, of course, there won't be time.

Somehow, I don't know how, but my heaven will have strutting peacocks, silly labradors, heavily scented flowers and turquoise seas. I will be able to *think* the most beautiful music that has ever been heard. I will be able to taste and smell things that create in me new capacities for joy. Somehow, in the heart and mind of God, there will be all the wonderful and good and beautiful things that have ever been. We will laugh, at first, at a distant half-remembered thought of death, but then we will forget even what and why it was. The end will have become the beginning, and the beginning will have become the everlasting *now*. The lost will all have been found: we will all have come home.

## The Divine Embrace

One morning this past summer, a friend and colleague phoned to discuss a variety of issues. There was a lot on his mind and we had a great deal of ground to cover. I was in the kitchen at the time he rang, and hurriedly I picked up the call on our cordless phone. I'd already been up for some hours and was very conscious of the amount of work I had to get through that day. Happily, it was a bright sunny day and during our conversation I wandered outside and sat on a bench in the sunlight.

Back inside the house one of my daughters and some of her young friends were baking cupcakes. All of a sudden, one of the little girls (whom I barely knew) came out of the kitchen door, launched herself onto my lap and threw her arms around me. I hugged her with my free arm and she leaned against me while I held her, all the while still talking on the telephone.

For the entire conversation, which lasted nearly a quarter of an hour, this child sat on my lap, her arms around my neck, leaning contentedly against me. Her spontaneous hug had an unexpected effect on me. As we both sat there, the sun bathing us in warmth, I could feel myself getting calmer and calmer. I have no idea whether my friend on the other end of the phone could sense a change in my voice or manner, but somehow he too became part of our embrace. I could feel myself relaxing and listening more carefully to what he was saying.

When we finally said goodbye, and my friend wished me well, I was overcome with a sense of tenderness and peace that pervaded me completely. My friend's caring words, the inexplicable love of the child on my lap, and the warmth of the sun all seemed to intertwine and flood me with a sense of well-being. After I got up I had a whole new perspective. My frenetic pace and racing mind had been altered, and the peace and deep joy I felt stayed with me for the rest of the day.

God's Spirit longs to reach out to us and draw us into the divine embrace. God is in the child throwing her arms around my neck. God is in the friend with the gentle words on the end of a phone. God is in the warmth of the sun. God is in the yearning we have for things to be different, to be better. In his song 'Train in the Distance' Paul Simon hints at this awareness, this deep longing, when he writes, 'The thought that life could be better, is woven indelibly into our hearts and our brains.' We know there is more.

This yearning defies simple explanation. It goes beyond wanting certain things, or even specific people and places. It is the tug in our hearts and the wrench in our stomachs that aches for we know not what. We accept, because scientists have told us so, that we only use one-tenth of our brains. We really have no idea what we could do if we were suddenly able to access the dormant nine-tenths. Could we see with God's eyes and hear with God's ears, the way George, the betting Yorkshireman, did? Perhaps that's the way it is with our souls and spirits, the bits of us we can't analyse. Perhaps we are only using a fraction of what we were originally created to use, and this sense of longing is a trenchant reminder that we were created to be and to live differently.

These feelings are not welcome guests. They bother us and unsettle us, and we whistle loudly to drown out their call. We run away into drink and drugs and hyperactivity. We stay away from silence. 'Why', we say to ourselves, 'if I am in control of my life, why can't I feel satisfied, feel full? Why is there this yearning for more?' And so we turn up the volume and cram the diary and hope against hope we will find something to make the feelings go away.

But the feelings won't go away, because they are nothing less than the Spirit of God looking for a way in, looking for a way to catch our attention and love us. The ache of longing we feel must be a tiny drop compared to the ache that God feels for us. We can turn from God and say 'no thank you, not today', but God cannot stop loving us. And so the heart of God continues to spill over with love for us, and we sometimes let ourselves feel a tiny bit, and even then we usually call it something else. But the nagging doubt persists, and we shove the untidy shirt-tails of our longing into our skirts and trousers, and vainly hope that no one will see the telltale signs that there is more to us, more to life, than we are happy to admit. *I'm all right, Jack! How about you?*

In order to open ourselves to God's love we have to get rid of some of the lies we've been telling ourselves about who we are and who God is. Some of us have been pretending that faith in God is all right for people who like that sort of thing, for little children and for old people. It can even be cool and trendy if it's a complicated, ritualistic way of life, as long as it happens in other countries to other people. We may laugh at the blatant showmanship and emotional excess of TV evangelists, and we steer clear of dodgy cults. *We're too clever to fall for that rubbish. It's all a con, isn't it?* But the longing carries on, the ache for something more, and when we've had all our holidays and parties, the free passes to the gym, and flown all the air miles, still we want more.

If we don't start acknowledging our need and looking for the love and truth that's trying to break into our lives, we will keep on experiencing disappointment and dis-ease. If we do not allow ourselves to accept what God is offering, we will always be let down. My friend Karina speaks of love wanting to break out of its vocabulary, wanting to explode into our lives all the time. She describes God having saturated everything on earth with his loving essence, and endowing everything we touch with loving opportunity. It is then up to us to take the opportunity, to see the possibilities, to catch God's vision of what life, ourselves and relationships can be like.

God is the Source, and if we don't go to the Source, our rivers and streams and pools of relief and satisfaction and pleasure will run dry. The unspoken, nameless yearning cannot be satisfied by anyone or anything but God. But part of the miracle of God is that, when we go to God, we also find new channels between us and other people opening up. Often, seeking God is to discover God's Spirit in new ways in those around us.

Alas, most of the time we would rather do it ourselves, try to solve our own problems, than admit that at the root of our problems lies a fractured relationship with the One who made us and the One who still and always loves us. We would rather bluff ourselves and suffer in the dark hours of the night than confess that we might feel a longing for God. We will spend countless amounts of time, money and energy convincing ourselves that our lives are full and complete, and that we don't need help from anyone else – especially God. We fear that a reliance on someone or something else will threaten and expose us, but that is to see God as an enemy. How differently might we see our situation if we could only imagine it from God's point of view.

Jennifer Rees Larcombe, my husband's cousin, recounts an extraordinary experience. She had been in hospital for several months, very ill and in severe pain. At one point she remembers the pain being so great that she shouted silently at Jesus that his intense suffering on the cross had only lasted six hours, but hers seemed to go on for ever. The answer she heard within astounded her. 'My suffering will go on until the last of my children are safely home, because I live in each cell of your physical bodies. I feel all your pain as you feel it, I also feel the pain of your broken hearts and the distress of your deranged minds. Please don't think I have separated myself from you.'[1] It was Michael Mayne, former Dean of Westminster, who observed that Jesus not only changes 'our idea of what God is and what we might become: he also changes our idea of what love is.'[2]

This is not the stance of a distant creator, but the position of One who is with us always, One who lives in us and aches for us in an intimacy we cannot fathom. In many services in many churches the minister says, 'The Lord is here,' and the congregation responds, 'His Spirit is with us.' But do we pause to think in what way God's Spirit is with us?

It is not as if God is a commodity with which we can be filled, the way we fill the tanks of our cars with petrol. It is not even as if God is present in parts of our beings, as if there are the God bits and then other, non-God bits. What Jennifer heard from Jesus, and what others have heard as well, is of a God who lives in us in a relationship of complete unity and intimacy.

At this point, words fail us. We step from image to analogy into mystery, and our minds run to keep up and then stop, while the Truth dances on ahead. We need to pay heed to our longing and acknowledge how strong and real it is, and try hard not to bury it under our pride and fear. We need to remember that Jesus' sojourn on earth was God's extravagant gift of himself, and that God has never withdrawn that gift. God *is* here, his Spirit *is* with us.

However, we have a choice. This God who aches to be one with us, who permeates our beings with his love, will never force our love, but asks, 'Will you let my love be shown, will you let my name be known, will you let my life be grown in you and you in me?'[3] God, above all others, knows what love is, and he will not settle for love that comes with one arm twisted behind its back. It is up to us to respond to God, but we will not have to go very far before God registers the movement we make towards him. This seems to be easier for some, and excruciating for others, but we all have our blind spots, the areas where we don't trust, where we are suspicious of God. But God is not playing huge practical jokes on us, of the 'now you see me, now you don't' variety. We have all been given the capacity for responding to God. We all have an awareness of that which is beyond what we can touch and see and hear. We are spiritual as well as physical beings.

If we look at Jesus and say only that he was a good role model, that is a step in the right direction. But as we try to follow his example we find that we can't. We cannot follow in his footsteps without his power, which was the power of the Holy Spirit. Also, we are left asking 'why?' if we do not run on Jesus' power. Why bother to turn the other cheek, walk the extra mile? Why bother to remain loyal to an unseen God, who asks the impossible? Why keep on loving when all your love is thrown back in your face and you are spat upon? Why bother with people who will not understand? The only way that Jesus can be a true role model is if we accept his explanations for why he did what he did, and who he was. Otherwise, it would be folly to follow him, a waste of our energies.

Jesus said, 'I am the vine, and you are the branches.' That describes an organic unity, being part of each other. But branches can only live by remaining as part of the vine. A branch cut off from the vine will wither and die. In Christ we have life, we have oneness and we know ourselves to be part of a spiritual body with Christ at the head.

That is what we are asked to do: stay connected to the vine and claim our identity as part of the vine. Not take on the job of saving the universe: that has already been done. Not vanquishing evil:

that has already been done. What we are asked to do is to 'let my love be shown'. We are to be living signposts of God's loving nature, living clues that God is a God of love. If life were one big mystery, and we were all detectives hunting for the answers, then how could we help each other to solve the mystery? That is what we can be for each other: we can help to solve the mystery of the universe by spreading God's love and living lives responding to God's love.

Jesus had free will: he chose to obey, to do what had to be done. He could see clearly enough what earthly existence was all about, and because he could see, he was willing to pay the price. Because of Jesus, we have a God who has experienced human existence, a God who has been human. When Jesus cried out from the cross, even though he had accepted it, he cried out as a wounded and dying human, 'Why have you forsaken me?' It was not a fancy rhetorical question. At that moment Jesus felt forsaken, all alone. Even though he had seen the vision of what most of us have forgotten, he could not see God then. It was faith that enabled him to say, 'It is finished. Into you hands I commit my spirit.'

Many people feel unloved, even if they have many friends or are married. If they cannot see God in the world, if they cannot open themselves to know God's love, then they will still feel the yearning, they will still hear the sound of a train in the distance, and they will wonder why. There is nothing more painful than feeling cut off from God's love, than having forgotten who we are and where we have come from. It is the bleakest and darkest sense of all. But remember, God has not cut us off. Our sense of alienation comes from our wandering away from God and refusing to see God, looking in other directions for other answers.

It is not easy to live in the awareness of God's love. For some reason it seems easier to live in a negative awareness, lugging around all our unforgiveness and pain. Even if we say we want to get rid of it, we often cling to it for dear life. Why is accepting God's forgiveness and forgiving ourselves and others so hard? It's hard because we form our identities on our unforgiven and hurting state, and to change it threatens our sense of security. We actually find it difficult to let go of the burden, whatever it is, and allow ourselves to be transformed into the new liberated person that God promises us we can be. The caterpillar cannot imagine the butterfly.

God bombards us with opportunities to see him and to be reminded of his transforming love, but we have put up defences against God and against the possibility of our freedom and ability to change. Because it is painful to let go of who we were, before we can see who we can be, we hold on to the negativity. We forget that all of life is a gift, that we are completely loved, and that we have so much to live for.

Letting go can be painful, but it is part of forgiveness and part of the joy of God's love. We have to let people go in order to be whole in God's love. Think of Jesus: he had to die in front of his mother. How difficult must that have been, when every fibre of his being must have wanted to protect her from such pain. But he was true to his relationship with God, and he had to let go of his relationships with other people. We need to learn to trust God so much that we are willing to leave those we love to God. Hopefully, we will not have to die the death of a martyr, the way some still do today, but we will have to die a type of death. We will have to die to our own will and our old understanding of God and of ourselves. We will have to stop acting as if we have to be careful with God, just in case, just in case he's out to get us. That is not the God we worship. We will have to die to old patterns of hatred, revenge, violence, cruelty and the insistence that we must be right.

In order to accept God's love we have to forgive ourselves or, rather, accept God's forgiveness for having been so blind. Whether we were blind by accident, or whether we refused to see is not important. What is important is that we can let go of our old ways and reach out to God and a new way of living. By choosing God, we can allow God's love to wipe out all the negativity we used to have. Then life becomes a challenge of *being love* wherever we go, on a moment-to-moment basis. We must not neglect splashing in the fountain!

One of the paradoxes in life is to accept the ache and longing for needs not met and love not returned by other people. We achieve nothing by pretending that things are the way we would like them to be, and we actually can make ourselves ill. But if we are honest with God, and hold on to the trust we have, then we can open ourselves to the peace that passes understanding. Remember, this is the God who is in every cell of our bodies, who aches when we ache and who only wants our good. Surely we can start to trust God a bit more?

If we desperately try to fill up the emptiness we feel inside with surrogates for spiritual love, we will only increase our emptiness and damage ourselves, but if we endure, and accept love from God, we will be filled. There are times in our lives when we cannot *make* certain things happen, and our only valid way forward is to accept that and hold on tightly to God. Remember, God knows, and God is with you.

No other human being is able to make us feel whole all the time, and if we look to someone else for our completeness, we will be let down, and we will only make them feel pressured. Yes, we definitely need human contact, human love and human touch – I have stressed the need for reaching out to other people and for forming close relationships – but no other human being can fill our deepest spiritual longings. We were created to be God's beloved, and there is an aspect of who we are that will never be fully satisfied by having only our physical and material needs met. This is what I mean about the sound of a train in the distance. It is not just a longing for another place, or another person, or another job (although it may be these as well), but a longing for spiritual wholeness.

I believe much time and energy is wasted and misspent because we do not know or believe this, or we have forgotten it. The way to this type of wholeness is the way to Love. It is not a head trip, but a voyage of the heart, and many of us have given our energies to our intellect instead of to our heart. Of course, we need to train and feed our minds; that is not the issue. The issue is whether we have forgotten that we were essentially created to love and to let ourselves be loved. Our wonderful and amazing brains are certainly part of us, but we cannot live fully if we only live in our heads. Our fullest identity lies in our belovedness, in the awareness that we were created *in* love and *for* love.

Erich Fromm wrote in *The Art of Loving* (Unwin, 1975) that 'The deepest need of man is the need to overcome separateness, to leave the prison of his aloneness.' If this is so, then how best do we overcome that aloneness? How best do we achieve meaningful union? How best can we transcend our own individuality and find at-one-ment? Strong, passionate, physical love gives us a glimpse, intimate friendship gives us a glimpse, but the best way we can know ourselves as not alone is if we accept our identity as children of God and experience the love of the Spirit.

It is this love that has the power to shape and complete us in the way that we were created to be shaped and made whole, as spiritual beings as well as physical bodies. If we allow ourselves to live in this love, we will be shaped more fully by God's idea of who we are and how best we can live. However, I am not advocating trying to live in a rarified spiritual atmosphere, not allowing ourselves to be sullied by physical imperatives. This is another of those mystifying paradoxes: the more engaged we are with other people, the more we open ourselves to all of life, the more we can sense and discover the living presence of the Holy Spirit. I often find that when I take school assemblies and spend time with young children I gain a new sense of God's extravagant love and tenderness, and our own vulnerability.

There will be times when we will need to come away, when we will need to detach our energies from too much busy-ness, but like Henri Nouwen in the community for the severely disabled, like Mother Teresa in the teeming streets of Calcutta, we will discover God in and among our earthly reality. We do not have to go somewhere else and do something else. *God is here, his Spirit is with us.*

There is a strange saying of Jesus in Luke 14:26: 'If anyone comes to me and does not hate his own father and mother and wife and children and brothers and sisters, yes, and even his own life, he cannot be my disciple.' The meaning of *hate* used here is not hate in an emotional sense, but implies the ability and willingness to be free from our own needs and desires. If we are not freed from what keeps us from following Christ, then we are in bondage and not living the lives to which we have been called.

We must 'risk the holy terror of living as if love really mattered'. This involves a type of holy terror, because it is so costly. Love is not a soft option; it is the choice of the brave, the obedient and the faithful. It takes a great amount of character and strength to risk opening ourselves to give and receive love, and to let go of our old falsely self-reliant way of living.

For me, being a Christian is a lot to do with taking risks, because it involves at its core entering a relationship where we are responding to One we cannot see, touch or hear, and yet One in whom we can have complete trust. All other humans, those we can see, touch and hear, will occasionally fail us. But God will never fail us. It is impossible for God to fail us, because God loves us completely. God never has an 'off' moment with us, or decides we are not worth the effort. Neither does God become angry with us the way we get angry with ourselves. In fact, anger is not part of what God feels for us: sorrow, pity, compassion, yes – but not anger. God may get angry at evil and cruelty, but not at us.

If we feel small and unworthy, is it because we are guilty about something and need to confess it, or is it because someone else has made us feel that way? God never makes us feel that way. If a little voice inside you is telling you how awful and worthless you are, you can be sure that it isn't God. Risk going to God and hearing his opinion of you. Even if you are in the wrong, God will never leave you without hope and without the offer of a restored relationship.

The biggest risk will be to accept that and to believe that God loves us completely and is always longing for closeness with us. This is the great mystery of our faith, that we did not choose God, but that God chose us.

> From all eternity we are hidden 'in the shadow of God's hand' and 'engraved on his palm.' Before any human being touches us, God 'forms us in secret' and 'textures us' in the depth of the earth, and before any human being decides about us, God 'knits us together in our mother's womb.' He loves us with a 'first' love, an unlimited, unconditional love, wants us to be his beloved children, and tells us to become as loving as himself.[4]

The risk is so demanding. Even Henri Nouwen admitted that

> for most of my life I have struggled to find God, to know God, to love God. I have tried hard to follow the guide-lines of the spiritual life – pray always, work for others, read the Scriptures – and to avoid the many temptations to dissipate myself. I have failed many times but always tried again, even when I was close to despair. Now I wonder whether I have sufficiently realised that during all this time God has been trying to find me, to know me, and to love me. The question is not 'How am I to find God?' but 'How am I to let myself be found by him?' The

question is not 'How am I to know God?' but 'How am I to let myself be known by God?' And, finally, the question is not 'How am I to love God?' but 'How am I to let myself be loved by God?' God is looking into the distance for me, trying to find me, and longing to bring me home.[5]

How would it change the way you thought of God if you could believe that he was looking for you, that as hard as you thought you were looking for him, he is seeking you with even more energy and compassion?

Ever since I was a child I have been aware of wanting to give God joy, of wanting to make God laugh, of wanting to make him glad that he created me. I have even been aware of wanting to *make* God love me and praise me for doing so well. While I believe that God aches to draw closer to each and every person, I also believe that God has no favourites. If I'm honest, there have been times when I wish he did, when I have wished I could earn his love and approval.

I know within myself there is a competitive streak that not only wants to please God, but that wants to please God more and better than anyone else he has created! I have had an unholy desire to be the best human being ever born, the jewel in God's human creation crown. But even this cannot cause God to turn away from me. Even my flawed response to God's gracious and all-encompassing love cannot stop that love.

If only we could accept down to our marrow that God loves us, then people like me would not feel they had to try so hard to win God's love. Perhaps we would not feel compelled to do so many cartwheels and juggling acts in order to catch God's eye. Perhaps we could be content to be who we have been created to be, and not compare ourselves with others, either favourably or unfavourably.

Perhaps we Divine-attention-seekers do not think too much of ourselves, but too little. Perhaps it is a lack of self-esteem that drives us to try to convince God of our worth. Even Henri Nouwen asked, 'Can I accept that I am worth looking for? Do I believe that there is a real desire in God simply to be with me?'[6] In his book about Rembrandt's painting of the story Jesus told about the prodigal son, Nouwen says:

> The parable of the prodigal son is a story that speaks about a love that existed before any rejection was possible and that will still be there after all rejections have taken place. It is the first and everlasting love of a God who is Father as well as Mother. It is the fountain of all true human love, even the most limited. Jesus' whole life and preaching had only one aim: to reveal this inexhaustible, unlimited motherly and fatherly love of his God and to show the way to let that love guide every part of our daily lives . . . It is the love that always welcomes home and always wants to celebrate.[7]

The good news is that we can know a measure of God's love and joy even while we are learning to come to know it more deeply. In the midst of our struggle, we can claim our identity as members of 'the household of God whose love is stronger than death and who empowers us to be in the world while already belonging to the kingdom of joy'.[8] We do not have to deny the struggle, but we can choose to live more in the awareness of the joy. We can trust that joy is more real than sorrow, that light is greater than darkness, and that the truth about life is greater than the passing reality of death. We can trust, as Noah did, in God's promise never to destroy again, and we can picture a rainbow of God's love encircling and enfolding all of creation in an everlasting embrace.

Will we ever come to the end of our voyage of discovery with God? Will we ever feel our search has ended?

> In one sense, it is finished when our hand, stretched out to God, feels the answering grasp and knows He is there. But in another sense the search never ends, for the first discovery is quickly followed by another, and that by another and so it goes on. To find that He IS is the mere starting point of our search. We are lured on to explore WHAT he is, and the search is never finished, and it grows more thrilling the further one proceeds.[9]

It is a case of rediscovering the everlasting arms, of remembering how our name sounds when spoken by our Lover. No one who has experienced God up close can ever be the same. It is as different as discussing aspects of physical attraction in a classroom and being wildly and wonderfully in love. Definitions, propositions, all words fly out of the window, and joy floods in. Let the joy flood in *now*. Eternity starts now for those living with the Holy Spirit in them. The divine spark is in all people, but when we say 'yes' to God, we open ourselves to a new way of being.

## The vision of love

I like how the contemporary French theologian Catherine LaCugna describes her vision of God's love for and involvement in all of creation:

> The living God is the God who is alive in relationship, alive in communion with the creature, alive with desire for union with every creature. God is so thoroughly involved in every last detail of creation that if we could truly grasp this it would altogether change how we approach each moment of our lives. For everything that exists – insect, agate, galaxy – manifests the mystery of the living God.[10]

Why? Why did God do it? Why did God cause the world to come into being, and humans to grow on it and look upwards into the heavens and say, 'There is more, there is more.' When Mother Julian asked the same question nearly six hundred years ago, she was given an amazingly simple answer. After her visions and all her years of meditating on God, this is what she was shown about God's meaning and purpose:

> From the time that it was shown I desired often to know what was our Lord's meaning. And fifteen years after and more, I was answered in inward understanding, saying, 'Would you know your Lord's meaning in this? Learn it well. Love was his meaning. Who showed it to you? Love. What did he show you? Love. Why did he show you? For love. Hold fast to this, and you shall learn and know more about love, but you will never need to know or understand about anything else for ever and ever.' Thus did I learn that love was our Lord's meaning.[11]

If love was Christ's meaning, then we can participate in Christ's continued presence on earth by living lives given over to expressing that love in ways which are freeing and healing for others, as well as for ourselves. Such a way of life will involve becoming vulnerable, allowing ourselves to be loved, and knowing that when drawing close to others we are also drawing closer to God. We can think of God as the Trinity – Father, Son and Holy Spirit – and remind ourselves that part of knowing and loving God is being in relationship. The first and most important relationship is with God, but that is lived out and discovered and expressed more fully in our relationships with others.

We can accept that our longing for sexual as well as spiritual experience springs from our deep, God-given yearning for wholeness. On every level, we ache to be whole, but lasting and complete wholeness is not possible apart from the life of the Spirit. We will also have to recognise that, while we live on planet earth, we will always know some alienation and longing.

But we are not meant to leave the dream and desire for heaven and the sweet by-and-by: we are to claim and experience what it means to be the Body of Christ, building the kingdom of God on earth *now*. There may well be a type of pie in the sky that we cannot know about until we die, but there is so much more that we can be doing to claim our inheritance *now* as the adopted children of a loving Father, who longs to live in us and make us whole in ways we cannot even imagine.

The hope we have that eternal life and everlasting love are possible is belief in the resurrection of Jesus Christ. Love was stronger than death then, and it remains so now, if we would only believe it and live it.

The huge joy is that we do not have to do it by ourselves. We have been given each other and the transforming, enlivening power of God's Holy Spirit. If we allow the power of God's love to have freedom in our lives, we will be amazed at what we can become. From time to time we have felt and seen what we, and all of life, can be like if we open the door to God. We try it God's way for a bit, and then, when we meet with resistance and failure, we give up on God and go back to our old ways of striving to do everything on our own – or worse, pretending that there never was another way of living.

We have all sinned and will sin again, for the rest of our lives, but that is not the final picture. We have been offered God's forgiveness and grace in a mysterious way by Jesus' death on the cross. When he rose from the dead on the third day it signalled the end of despair and alienation, and ushered in a new way for us to live.

Living in Christ means accepting what he did, and refusing to let go of the dream of eventual wholeness and completeness, for us as individuals and for all of creation. That's one of God's promises. Either we accept it, and live as if it is true, or we sink back into a pattern of seeing ourselves adrift in a hostile universe. Our confidence comes from our faith in God, not from what we hope *we* will be able to do. Our performance may be important, even crucial at times, but what is even more important is whether or not our hearts remain open to God. The most important thing is to see ourselves as belonging to God and caught up in what God is doing. We can either respond by saying 'yes' to God, or by trying to go it alone, even though that is bound to fail. So many of our problems and frustrations come from the fact that we have lost sight of who we are and the true mystery of our existence.

### Being the image of God

Along with Mother Julian and so many others, I have come to believe that love was the sum of our Lord's meaning. I have come to accept that there is nothing higher or better in all of creation. My understanding of love, which is, of course, continually unfold-ing and changing, has given rise to a vision of how I think we are meant to live.[12]

My vision of what we humans can become, even while we inhabit our imperfect bodies in our imperfect world, sometimes glows brightly and I am filled with energy and hope. I offer you my vision, hoping that it will inspire you, above all, to open yourself to God and allow yourself to be drawn closer to the One in whom we find ourselves and each other and in whom we will one day be whole.

If we accept that we are made in the image of a God who longs for justice, who yearns to love and be loved, who aches for peace and wholeness in a world created to be joyous and beautiful and among people imbued with God's Spirit, we will begin to live in a different way.

We will take time to rediscover the rhythms of nature, bestow dignity and value on mothers and motherhood, as well as on fathers and fatherhood; we will see that caring for the earth and all created things is what true dominion means. Our confidence in the God of love will inspire us to love ourselves and others, and we will begin to take down the tangled barbed-wire fences of alienation, fear and hatred between Us and Them.

We will resist war and killing because we will recognise that life is sacred, and that forgiveness, reconciliation and healing is possible, and that as friends of Christ it is our duty as well as our joy to bring these about. Our highest calling, irrespective of what jobs or roles or other responsibilities we have, will be to live in the active loving service of Christ.

We will stand out as those who have hope in the midst of darkness, and, because of our hope, the darkness will be diminished and will ultimately be brought into the light. We will be confident and creative because we know who we are: neither worms nor angels, but people made by God to become one with God in love.

We will understand that every galloping horse, every glint of vibrant feather and flash of sleek fin, every creature at play, can give us a glimpse of God, can show us another facet of an infinite Creator who is infinitely creative and loving. We will worship the Creator and not the created, neither ourselves nor other creatures. Once again, our bodies will become temples of the Holy Spirit, instead of objects of shame, subjects of violence or icons of lust.

We will be able to reach out to others, but we will not sin in our touching. We will lose ourselves in acts of love, but we will never lose our individuality nor allow others to rob us of our dignity and sense of identity.

Our hands will help and heal, comfort and protect, soothe and calm, excite and arouse, but they will not hurt or damage, steal or invade, expose or stifle, frighten or threaten.

Our words will give hope and courage, and our actions will bring about justice and peace. Though our bodies need to eat and sleep, and will eventually die, our spirits will be strong and steady, wise and alert. In our lives and in all our actions, we will depend on the continual presence of the loving, healing, liberating Spirit of God.

We will know and live in the truth of what Paul discovered when he wrote, 'Now the Lord is the Spirit, and where the Spirit of the Lord is, there is freedom. And we all, with unveiled face, beholding the glory of the Lord, are being changed into his likeness from one degree of glory to another; for this comes from the Lord who is the Spirit' (2 Corinthians 3:17–18). One day we will be free, and we will know ourselves as we are known: the beloved made in the image of the One who is Love, held for ever in the Divine Embrace.

**Introduction**
1. Gabrielle Cox, 'Thought for the Day', BBC Radio 4, 11 August 1998.

**1: In the Beginning**
1. John Polkinghorne, *Science and Creation* (SPCK, 1988), p. 97.
2. Peter Millar, 'The Time Machine' in *The Sunday Times Magazine*, 24 March 1996.
3. *The Dart of Longing Love: Daily Readings from The Cloud of Unknowing and The Epistle of Privy Counsel*, rendered into modern English with an introduction by Robert Llewelyn (Darton, Longman & Todd, 1983), p. 14.
4. Bishop Richard Holloway, quoted in the *Church Times*, 27 December 1996, p. 3.
5. Polkinghorne, *Science and Creation*, p. 51.
6. ibid. pp. 49–50.
7. ibid. p. 63.
8. ibid. p. 62.
9. Facts from Brennan Manning, *The Ragamuffin Gospel* (Scripture Press, 1990).

**2: Partners in the Dance**
1. John Polkinghorne, *Science and Creation* (SPCK, 1988), p. 66.
2. Dietrich Bonhoeffer, *Letters and Papers from Prison* (SCM Press, 1953), pp. 164, 166.
3. John Austin Baker, *The Foolishness of God* (Darton, Longman & Todd, 1970), p. 406.
4. Dame Cicely Saunders in a sermon at Great Saint Mary's, Cambridge.
5. Peter Selby, *BeLonging – Challenge to a Tribal Church* (SPCK, 1991), p. 32.
6. Julian of Norwich, *Enfolded in Love: Daily Readings with Julian of Norwich* (Darton, Longman & Todd, 1980), p. 35.

### 3: Who Am I?

1. Jane Williams, *Trinity and Unity* (Darton, Longman & Todd), p. 18.
2. Henri Nouwen, *The Path of Peace* (Darton, Longman & Todd, 1995), pp. 22, 23.
3. Quoted in Shelagh Brown and Phil Lawson Johnston, *Value Me* (Bible Reading Fellowship, 1995), pp. 7–8.

### 4: How Then Shall We Live?

1. Diane Ackerman, *A Natural History of the Senses* (Random House, 1990), p. 73.
2. Madeleine L'Engle, *Walking on Water* (Harold Shaw Publishers, 1980), p. 60.

### 5: The Smile Within

1. Julian of Norwich, *Enfolded in Love: Daily Readings with Julian of Norwich* (Darton, Longman & Todd, 1980), p. 31.
2. Quoted in Madeleine L'Engle, *Walking on Water* (Harold Shaw Publishers, 1980), p. 31.

### 6: When It All Goes Wrong

1. Madeleine L'Engle, *Walking on Water* (Harold Shaw Publishers, 1980), p. 190.
2. Philip J. Newell, *Echo of the Soul* (Canterbury Press, 2000), p. 62.
3. Julian of Norwich, *Enfolded in Love: Daily Readings with Julian of Norwich* (Darton, Longman & Todd, 1980), p. 55.
4. Quoted in Doug Shadel and Bill Thatcher, *The Power of Acceptance* (Newcastle Publishing Company, 1997), p. 238.
5. Louise Hay, *You Can Heal Your Life* (Eden Grove Editions, 1984), p. 52.
6. The words of the Dismissal, *The Alternative Service Book 1980*, p. 145.

### 7: Love in Action

1. Printed on a prayer card and taken from *Words to Love By* (Ave Maria Press, 1985).
2. John Tinsley, *Bishop John* (Three Crowns, 1985), p. 22.
3. National WATCH leaflet, from WATCH, St John's Church, Waterloo Road, London SE1 8TY.
4. Miroslav Volf, *Exclusion and Embrace* (Abingdon Press, 1996), p. 167.

### 8: When God Calls

1. Quoted in *Voices of This Calling: Experiences of the First Generation of Women Priests*, ed. Christina Rees (SCM-Canterbury Press, 2002), p. 101.
2. ibid. p. 66.

3. Quoted in Doug Shadel and Bill Thatcher, *The Power of Acceptance* (Newcastle Publishing Company), p. 238.

4. Quoted in Gerald Priestland, *Priestland's Progress* (BBC Publications, 1981), p. 200.

5. Madeleine L'Engle, *Walking on Water* (Harold Shaw Publishers, 1980), p. 195.

## 9: Being There

1. Christopher Collingwood, *The Divine Dance of Love* (Canterbury Press, 1996), p. 12.

2. Elisabeth Moltmann-Wendel, *I Am My Body* (SCM Press, 1994), p. 104.

3. William Countryman, *The Truth About Love* (SPCK, 1993), p. 42.

4. Shelagh Brown and Phil Lawson Johnston, *Value Me* (Bible Reading Fellowship, 1995), pp. 44–5.

5. John V. Taylor, *A Matter of Life and Death* (SCM Press, 1986), pp. 73–4.

6. Henri Nouwen, *The Path of Peace* (Darton, Longman & Todd, 1995), p. 35.

7. ibid. p. 41.

8. ibid. p. 43.

9. Story told in ibid. pp. 45–6.

## 10: A Mutual Delight

1. Thomas Moore, *SoulMates* (HarperCollins, 1994), pp. 184–5.

2. ibid. p. 183.

3. Elaine Storkey, *The Search for Intimacy* (Hodder & Stoughton, 1995), p. 207.

4. Carter Heyward, *Touching Our Strength* (HarperCollins, 1989), p. 4.

5. ibid. p. 94.

6. ibid. p. 109.

## 12: The Divine Embrace

1. *Day by Day with God: May to August 1999*, ed. Mary Reid (Bible Reading Fellowship/Christina Press, 1999).

2. Michael Mayne, *A Year Lost and Found* (Darton, Longman & Todd, 1987), p. 55.

3. John Bell and Graham Maule, in their hymn, 'The Summons', Iona Community.

4. Henri Nouwen, *The Return of the Prodigal Son* (Darton, Longman & Todd, 1992), p. 106.

5. ibid. p. 106.

6. ibid. p. 107.

7. ibid. p. 109.

8. ibid. pp 116–17.

9. Isobel Kuhn, in Kathy Keay (ed.), *Dancing on Mountains* (HarperCollins, 1996), p. 154.

10. Catherine LaCugna, *God for Us* (HarperSanFrancisco, 1991), p. 304.

11. Julain of Norwich, *Enfolded in Love: Daily Readings with Julian of Norwich* (Darton, Longman & Todd, 1980), p. 59.

12. Much of this section is taken from 'In what way are we made in the image of God?', my thesis for a master's degree from King's College, London, August 1998, pp. 50–1.

# BIBLIOGRAPHY

Ackerman, Diane, *A Natural History of the Senses* (Random House, 1990).

Baker, John Austin, *The Foolishness of God* (Darton, Longman & Todd, 1970).

Bonhoeffer, Dietrich, *Letters and Papers from Prison* (SCM Press, 1953).

Brown, Shelagh and Johnston, Phil Lawson, *Value Me* (Bible Reading Fellowship, 1995).

Collingwood, Christopher, *The Divine Dance of Love* (Canterbury Press, 1996).

Countryman, William, *The Truth About Love* (SPCK, 1993).

Davis Kasl, Charlotte, *Finding Joy* (HarperCollins, 1994).

Hay, Louise, *You Can Heal Your Life* (Eden Grove Editions, 1984).

Heyward, Carter, *Touching Our Strength* (HarperCollins, 1989).

Julian of Norwich, *Enfolded in Love: Daily Readings with Julian of Norwich* (Darton, Longman & Todd, 1980).

Keay, Kathy (ed.), *Dancing on Mountains* (HarperCollins, 1996).

L'Engle, Madeleine, *Walking on Water* (Harold Shaw Publishers, 1980).

LaCugna, Catherine, *God for Us* (HarperSanFransisco, 1991).

Llewelyn, Robert (ed.), *The Dart of Longing Love: Daily Readings from The Cloud of Unknowing and The Epistle of Privy Counsel* (Darton, Longman & Todd, 1983).

Manning, Brennan, *The Ragamuffin Gospel* (Scripture Press, 1995).

Mayne, Michael, *A Year Lost and Found* (Darton, Longman & Todd, 1987).

Moltmann-Wendel, Elisabeth, *I Am My Body* (SCM Press, 1994).

Moore, Thomas, *SoulMates* (HarperCollins, 1994).

Newell, J. Philip, *Echo of the Soul* (Canterbury Press, 2000).

Nouwen, Henri, *The Path of Peace* (Darton, Longman & Todd, 1995).

Nouwen, Henri, *The Path of Power* (Darton, Longman & Todd, 1995).

Nouwen, Henri, *The Return of the Prodigal Son* (Darton, Longman & Todd, 1994).

Peck, M. Scott, *In Search of Stones* (Simon & Schuster, 1990).

Polkinghorne, John, *Science and Creation* (SPCK, 1988).

Priestland, Gerald, *Priestland's Progress* (BBC Publications, 1981).

Rees, Christina (ed.), *Voices of This Calling: Experiences of the First Generation of Women Priests* (SCM-Canterbury Press, 2002).

Reid, Mary (ed.), *Day by Day with God: May–August 1999* (Bible Reading Fellowship and Christina Press, 1999).

Selby, Peter, *BeLonging* (SPCK, 1991).

Shadel, Doug and Thatcher, Bill, *The Power of Acceptance* (Newcastle Publishing Company, 1997).

Storkey, Elaine, *The Search for Intimacy* (Hodder & Stoughton, 1995).

Taylor, John V., *A Matter of Life and Death* (SCM Press, 1986).

Tinsley, John, *Bishop John* (Three Crowns, 1985).

Williams, Jane, *Trinity and Unity* (Darton, Longman & Todd, 1995).